SAY IT

LIVE IT

OTHER BOOKS BY LARRY KAHANER

NONFICTION

Cults That Kill
On the Line
The Phone Book (coauthor)

FICTION

Naked Prey (under the pseudonym Larry Kane)

SAY IT & LIVE IT

50 CORPORATE MISSION STATEMENTS THAT HIT THE MARK

PATRICIA JONES and
LARRY KAHANER

CURRENCY

DOUBLEDAY

NEW YORK LONDON TORONTO SYDNEY AUCKLAND

A CURRENCY BOOK
PUBLISHED BY DOUBLEDAY
a division of Bantam Doubleday Dell Publishing Group, Inc.
1540 Broadway, New York, New York 10036

CURRENCY and DOUBLEDAY are trademarks of Doubleday,
a division of Bantam Doubleday Dell Publishing Group, Inc.

Book design by Chris Welch

Library of Congress Cataloging-in-Publication Data
Jones, Patricia, 1954–
    Say it & live it : 50 corporate mission
    statements that hit the mark / Patricia Jones
    and Larry Kahaner.
        p.   cm.
        1. Mission statements.   I. Kahaner, Larry.
    II. Title.
    HD30.285.J66   1995
    658.4′012—dc20   95-5705
                                          CIP

ISBN 0-385-47630-2

1 3 5 7 9 10 8 6 4 2

DEDICATED TO JESSE MARLOWE,
OUR MISSION

Contents

Road Maps for the High Road

A recent study of twenty-five "corporate tools" such as customer surveys, pay-for-performance, total quality management, and reengineering, which showed that managers used mission statements more than any other tool. The 1994 survey by Bain & Company and The Planning Forum also noted that when managers were asked to list tools in which they were "extremely satisfied," mission statements had more votes than any other tool.

Managers like mission statements because they make a difference in whether a company succeeds or fails.

Corporate mission statements—sometimes called value statements, credos, or principles—are the operational, ethical, and financial guiding lights of companies. They are not simply mottoes or slogans; they articulate the goals, dreams, behavior, culture, and strategies of companies more than any other document.

During our research one fact stood out. It was how much companies truly relied on their mission statements to help them through trying times and in making tough decisions. The comment we heard over and over was: "We didn't need long discussions about how we were going to handle the situation. The mission statement quickly told us how to act."

We found successful, exciting, and powerful companies that had true values. Their mission statements were not just concepts and philosophies they had cobbled together but were well-thought-out ideas that had helped them meet and exceed their financial dreams, treat their employees well, break free of a crisis, and stake out a piece of "the right thing to do." They were road maps for the high road.

Corporate mission statements show us the best in corporate America. They are lofty values and ideals that are worthy of study, thought, and emulation. Refreshingly, they show us a side of corporations that many of us never knew existed—the human side, the emotional side, the values-based side.

We, the authors, think of mission statements somewhat as we do the U.S. Constitution. This document promises a fair trial, for instance, but we all know that doesn't always happen. Injustice exists. The Constitution is also fallible. The original document didn't outlaw slavery. Still, the Constitution is an excellent, much revered, and often imitated set of values. It allows us to aim high and set worthy goals.

These ideals are what mission statements are all about—worthy goals and aspirations. Sometimes you reach them and sometimes you don't, but you always try because it's the right thing to do.

The companies chosen for this book passed two tests. First, they have well-written, well-focused, compelling, or unique mission statements, values, philosophies, visions, or whatever they call them. Second, they try to live up to them.

We discovered that many companies we interviewed wrote or rewrote their mission statement during the 1980s when they were being reengineered, downsized, restructured, or otherwise radically altered. Quite simply, they needed a new philosophy to cope with a changing business climate, which included awareness of cultural diversity, worker empowerment, globalization, environmental stewardship, total quality, teamwork, and emphasis on the customer. Mission statements were being used as a tool to "gather the troops" and effect a new corporate culture or behavior.

We also were impressed at how passionate company officials were about their mission statements. They were truly proud of what they had done and how they were using these documents. In most cases, people were quite willing to talk to us because it meant a lot to them.

Then there were those companies that wouldn't talk to us at all. These companies had mission statements—pretty good ones, we thought—but they wouldn't grant us an interview. At first, we couldn't understand why they were unwilling to discuss something positive about themselves. What we surmised was that although these companies had mission statements, they didn't truly live them—or try to live them. The last thing management wanted was for their employees to see them quoted in a book about how the company lives up to these ideals, while everyone at the company knows differently. Obviously, these companies didn't make the book.

We are certain that the companies that cooperated with us—companies whose senior officials spent time discussing their mission statements and how they were used—truly employed their mission statements as advertised. They're confident that those throughout the company won't snicker when they read management's comments.

We were gratified at the high level of interest our inquiries received. More than half of our interviews were with chairmen, CEOs, COOs, presidents, and people of that stratum. Indeed, this signaled to us immediately how strongly these companies felt about their values and principles.

We were also intrigued by how many of the companies we spoke to have been chosen as great places to work in such books as *The 100 Best Companies to Work For in America*. This was coincidental, but in retrospect we shouldn't have been surprised. These companies demonstrated through their mission statements how important employees were to the companies' success.

Many of the companies profiled here also turned out to be industry leaders, companies that have the lion's share of a market or produce the best in their industry. Also not surprising—when we look back at it —was how many companies, five to be exact, have been winners of the prestigious Malcolm Baldrige National Quality Award, established by Congress in 1987 and given by the Department of Commerce for quality management. (Some have been two-time winners.)

We were taken aback by the number of companies that were in the process of writing or rewriting their mission statements. Several told us to try them again for the next edition.

To sum up, we found the companies that truly lived their mission statements were hands-down winners in many different areas. This correlation showed us time after time how mission statements can make a difference.

In most instances we either reproduced the mission statement exactly as it's presented or simply copied the mission statement word for word. It seemed to us that some statements benefited more by exact reproduction than others.

In some cases, though, we didn't include all parts of a company's mission statement. Sometimes we skipped the obvious—"We will be the best widget company in the world, blah, blah, blah"—and in rare instances we were forced to cut the mission statement because it was too long. We apologize for taking these liberties.

In the following pages you'll see what's right about American business. You'll also learn, by example, how to write a mission statement for your company, even if it's a small company. In fact, we included a few small-company profiles just so you could see that their mission statements aren't really different from those of the industry giants. At the end of this book you'll find a section giving tips on writing your own mission statement, with ideas taken from the companies profiled herein.

We would like to acknowledge the help we received from all the companies we interviewed, especially from those people in the corporate office whose time is limited. We thank them for giving us permission to reproduce their mission statements, which, of course, remain their copyrighted property. We would also like to thank our agent, Gordon Kato at ICM, who recognized this new business trend immediately, and Lynn Fenwick at Currency Doubleday, who embraced the idea when it was presented.

Patricia Jones and Larry Kahaner
Alexandria, Virginia
November 1994

AT&T

Our Common Bond

WE COMMIT TO THESE VALUES TO GUIDE
OUR DECISIONS AND BEHAVIOR

RESPECT FOR INDIVIDUALS

We treat each other with respect and dignity, valuing individual and cultural differences. We communicate frequently and with candor, listening to each other regardless of level or position. Recognizing that exceptional quality begins with people, we give individuals the authority to use their capabilities to the fullest to satisfy their customers. Our environment supports personal growth and continuous learning for all AT&T people.

DEDICATION TO HELPING CUSTOMERS

We truly care for each customer. We build enduring relationships by understanding and anticipating our customers' needs and by serving them better each time than the time before. AT&T customers can count on us to consistently deliver superior products and services that help them achieve their personal or business goals.

HIGHEST STANDARDS OF INTEGRITY

We are honest and ethical in all our business dealings, starting with how we treat each other. We keep our promises and admit our mistakes. Our personal conduct ensures that AT&T's name is always worthy of trust.

INNOVATION

We believe innovation is the engine that will keep us vital and growing. Our culture embraces creativity, seeks different perspectives and risks pursuing new opportunities. We create and rapidly convert technology into products and services, constantly searching for new ways to make technology more useful to customers.

TEAMWORK

We encourage and reward both individual and team achievements. We freely join with colleagues across organizational boundaries to advance the interests of customers and shareowners. Our team spirit extends to being responsible and caring partners in the communities where we live and work.

BY LIVING THESE VALUES, AT&T ASPIRES TO SET A STANDARD OF EXCELLENCE WORLDWIDE THAT WILL REWARD OUR SHAREOWNERS, OUR CUSTOMERS, AND ALL AT&T PEOPLE.

A Crash Course in Corporate Change

There it was in black and white. Bob Allen, the chairman of AT&T, wrote an introduction to the 1993 annual report stating that the company had made a mistake.

"Because our long distance network was so highly computerized, we thought customers would jump at the chance to buy computers from us." He continued: "We were wrong, and finally we merged with an established computer company, NCR, which was recently named AT&T Global Information Services."

To those unfamiliar with the corporate culture of AT&T, admitting mistakes is not something the telecommunications giant is good at. In fact, before the famous divestiture in 1984—in which AT&T sprung loose the local Bell telephone companies in exchange for the right to enter new, unregulated businesses such as computers—saying that you made an error was like confessing that you had committed a homicide. After all, you were the matriarch of all American businesses: Ma Bell. The corporate culture and employee behavior just didn't allow for imperfection. Indeed, for AT&Ters to even be humble about *anything* went against the corporate fabric.

However, since Allen took the helm in 1988, AT&T has been on a crash course to change their corporate culture and image—to be less arrogant, more attuned to customers' needs, and more service oriented.

And their *Our Common Bond*, penned by Allen with employee help, is the company's compass.

Marilyn Laurie, the senior vice president of employee information who led the mission statement task force, says: "In 1989, Bob Allen had decided that in order for business to be effective it would have to be better focussed on customers." That led to a restructuring into separate business units that in turn traumatized many AT&Ters who weren't used to any kind of changes in the company. This was a heavily regulated company that had never changed its culture in its almost hundred-year history. "It didn't take very long before people started asking: 'What's the glue that holds us together? Are we just a holding company? What do we have in common?'"

The company was literally in turmoil as business units and divisions went about the tasks of resizing their work forces and adjusting costs to compete in their individual market segments. Without the revenues from the cash cow of the local phone companies to help the bottom line, AT&T had to be competitive in an industry in which it was used to being the sole player. In the new world of telecommunications, there were competitors like Sprint and MCI to handle.

Everything at the company—and in the industry in general—was changing so fast that Allen felt that AT&T needed something that would stay the same. It needed an anchor. "It needed a counterbalance to the splitting of company into units," says Laurie. Allen wrote an early version, *Our Common Bond—A Direction for AT&T*, on a yellow pad, and, with the help of Laurie's task force, tested it throughout the company.

"Bob never rushed the process," says Laurie. "He didn't want it to be the slogan of the month. He didn't want it to be a banner. He wanted it to be a real vehicle for culture change." The process of writing, rewriting, and testing took more than two years.

"In the original values, the 'teamwork' section didn't appear and, on the advice of employees, Allen decided to put it into the revised edition. Also, in the original text 'quality' was a separate category, but we decided that quality had to be integrated into each value. Quality is important in the way we approach everything we do," says Laurie.

Many company mission statements devote a special section to serving shareholder interests. However, Allen and his employees decided to leave it out because they considered it a "given" that shareholders would be served if everything else went according to *Our Common Bond*.

Another major change that came from employees was the section *Respect for Individuals*. One of the lines, **We communicate frequently and with candor, listening to each other regardless of level or position,** would have been unimaginable before divestiture. AT&T

was a bureaucratic, top-down kind of place with almost a military air about it.

When asked by a writer for a company magazine about whether the first value, respect for individuals, will actually change anything at AT&T, he replied: "Not because it's on a piece of paper. It has the potential to really have an impact on the company, on the people, on the way we treat our customers—but only if we live the values and have them as a constant reminder, in the mirror, when we're weighing decisions. And it begins with me," Allen said, "it begins with my relationship with the people who work with me."

One day Allen would like to say that everyone at AT&T lives *Our Common Bond*, but that day is not yet here. He says, "We won't live by those values one hundred percent anytime soon, but our intent is to move in that direction."

Allen and others note that there is skepticism among employees about *Our Common Bond* and whether AT&T can live up to its principles. In fact, a 1991 survey showed that only one in five of AT&T's employees thought top management's statements were for real.

"*Our Common Bond* is meant to be aspirational," says Laurie. "The bar was set very high. There is no expectation that we would be living it yet.

"This is a multiyear project, to build the company around these values. As recently as 1994, we had strategy forums for executive level managers who discussed strategy and its relationship to *Our Common Bond* so we could have a common agreement and understanding as to why they think it's necessary."

It all has to do with changing the corporate culture and the behavior of its managers and employees. Allen says: "There's plenty of evidence to demonstrate that we have a lot of work to do. And we know a lot of skeptical people will see the values statement for the first time and say, 'Well, the words and intent are terrific, but I don't see that kind of behavior around here.'"

Notes Laurie: "We're at the stage where people quote it a lot. It's a rare meeting where it doesn't come up. It's a watermark. We're making more progress on some points than on others.

"There's a lot of humility in the distance between the expression of values and where we are now. We still have a long way to go," she says.

In his introduction to the annual report where Allen discusses AT&T's miscalculation of its foray into the computer industry, the chairman was walking the walk for everyone to see. "We keep our promises and admit our mistakes," states *Our Common Bond*.

Allen did just that.

Hanna Andersson

Our Purpose

In partnership with our customers, we will provide products to enhance the richly textured experience of family and community. We celebrate this experience through the integrity of our merchandise, and our respect for the values we share with our customers. Our culture bears witness to our beliefs.

Values

RESPECT

Recognizing and acknowledging the value and contribution of each person or endeavor. Acting with respect means treating others as you want to be treated.

INTEGRITY

Being true to your values and honest about your commitment to them.

RESPONSIBILITY

Being accountable for your actions and obligations, as a company and as individuals.

"Welcome to Hanna"
Ways to Grow and Participate

1. Be kind and intelligent with others, especially our customers. Respect, responsibility and integrity make good things happen.

2. Bring energy to your work. Big or small, if a task needs to be done, it needs to be done well. Think of each action in terms of how it strengthens Hanna.

3. Understand that learning prompts change. Together, they are the stepping stones to the evolution of our business.

4. Office politics take energy away from important work and divide rather than unite. It is work, and not talk, that matters.

5. When possible, plan your time off around the work flow. A balance between home life and Hanna is healthy and encouraged.

6. The Hanna environment should be clean, healthy and comfortable for everyone. Keep your work area organized and tidy. It is your job to pick up after yourself.

7. Your participation is encouraged. Learn as much as you can about your job, the company and our industry so that you may grow with us.

8. Hanna is sensitive to the actions and concerns of the community and the world around us. Avenues for social service and awareness are available to all.

9. We will all share in the success we create.

10. Laughter sees us through the day. Have fun.

Delicate prose for tough clothes.

Gun Denhart and her husband, Tom, started Hanna Andersson in 1984 because they were both dissatisfied with the poor quality of children's clothing in the United States. Denhart grew up in Sweden, where she had seen high quality children's clothing, and decided to sell them in the States. After contacting a Swedish manufacturer and naming the company after her grandmother, Hanna Andersson was established.

They produced the first catalog on their kitchen table. To demonstrate the quality of the fabric, they painstakingly glued one-inch-by-one-inch swatches to each catalog, crossed their fingers, and mailed 75,000 catalogs. That was February 1984. By the end of the first six months they had sold $53,000 worth of clothing; after the first year they sold $200,000, and after the second year $1.5 million. By 1993 Hanna Andersson had become a highly respected mail order firm, sending 15 million catalogs annually—four issues a year—and employing 292 people. Sales exceeded $44 million, and the company was starting to reach out into the retail market.

It's not surprising to find the phrase **the integrity of our merchandise** in *Our Purpose*, the Hanna Andersson corporate mission statement. To emphasize the point that their clothes last a long time, the company began a program called Hannadowns in 1985, still a major focus of the company today. The catalogs explain the program and invite customers to participate. Simply put, customers can return their outgrown Hannas for a 20 percent credit of the original purchase price which can be used toward future purchases. The company then donates the returned clothes to needy women and children. As many as 10,000 items a month have been received.

Our Purpose is carefully worded to reflect their industry and vision. "The part . . . **to enhance the richly textured experience of family and community** passed the goose-pimple test," says Gun Denhart, founder and CEO of Hanna Andersson. "It felt wonderful." This belief is manifested in the company donating five percent of its profits to charities chosen by employees, who are encouraged to be active in charitable causes. The company will match each employee's charitable contributions up to $500 per year. Hanna Andersson pays 50 percent of their employees' child care costs and thought about installing an on-site child care center. After surveying their employees, they decided to keep the present plan in place and give their employees the flexibility in their own child care arrangements. Eighty-one percent of employees are women, so this is a very important issue for the company.

The last line of *Our Purpose* reads: **Our culture bears witness to our beliefs.** "It was written because we want to live the way we say we live. We don't want hypocrisy. It's meant to keep each other in line," says Denhart.

But all this success took a toll. Denhart and her husband, Tom, who both quit their high pressure, rat race careers eleven years earlier, were seriously looking at getting out of the business.

"This created a lot of talk around the company and people were nervous," says Denhart, "but we decided to stay with it and recommit to success."

The dilemma is a common one in fast-growing companies: management losing touch with the expanding number of employees.

"We couldn't touch everyone every day anymore, but we wanted to express how we wanted the company to act and feel. So we developed ten points entitled *How to Be Happy at Hanna, Our Purpose*, and a *Values* statement. We update these three philosophies regularly." The couple took all middle managers offsite for a day and a half of meetings to discuss the strategic plans for the company. They revised *Our Purpose, Values*, and *How to Be Happy at Hanna*.

The philosophies took on a more mature tone, reflecting the company's growth and stability. "We took it from a baby company to a teenage company," Denhart remembers. "The statement is not as inspirational as the old one, but is more serious for serious times."

Their *Values* statement, for example, became more succinct and changed from **Respect, Integrity,** and **Fairness** to **Respect, Integrity,** and **Responsibility.** "We felt *responsibility*—fiscally and to the employees and customers—was a better word," Denhart says. "We now have self-directed teams; we got rid of the hierarchy. In the phone room, for instance, each operator now has the authority to resolve customer concerns on the spot."

When the offsite meeting was completed, each middle manager met with their departments and explained the new mission statement and offered the opportunity for input. "About seventy-five percent of the employees gave input," says Denhart. Out of these efforts, the *How to Be Happy at Hanna* evolved into *"Welcome to Hanna" Ways to Grow and Participate.*

And what about that tenth add-on point in **"Welcome to Hanna,"** the part that says **Laughter sees us through the day. Have fun?** Denhart adds: "They could come up with only nine points this time, and so I added the tenth."

Managers can stop employees in the hall and ask them to recite or express an understanding or knowledge of the new philosophies. If they can, they get a button that says "I know it." The button is redeemable for a five-dollar credit in the company cafeteria.

AVIS.

The Avis Quest For Excellence

At Avis Rent A Car, our business is renting cars; our mission is total customer satisfaction.

Our goal is to provide the best quality customer service: to treat each customer the way we ourselves want to be treated. To exceed our customer's expectations.

We believe that only by maximizing our service and our productivity can we maximize our employee equity and our profits.

We are dedicated to a vigorous program of self-evaluation and improvement.

We continually strive to provide better and innovative services to enhance the travel experience for our customers. We work to strengthen our bonds with all active participants in the delivery of our service: our customers, our suppliers, and our co-workers in all areas.

We know that total customer service and satisfaction require the team effort of all employees, at all times.

"We try harder."

VISION STATEMENT

AVIS WILL BE RECOGNIZED AS THE PREEMINENT COMPANY IN THE RENT-A-CAR INDUSTRY IN THE AREAS OF:

- CUSTOMER SERVICE AND SATISFACTION
- EMPLOYEE PARTICIPATION
- RETURN TO SHAREHOLDERS

VALUE STATEMENTS
CUSTOMER SATISFACTION

Total customer satisfaction is Avis' goal.

Fulfilling customer needs is the prime reason for our company's existence. All employee-owners have a responsibility to satisfy customer expectations through quality of service, in a manner which will encourage long-term customer relationships.

We will strive to provide the highest quality service to our internal and external customers, consistent with our shareholder objectives.

We will look to continuously improve how the customer views Avis by seeking "moments of opportunity" where we can exceed their expectations.

The Voice of the People

Avis is the world's second largest car rental company—the "We Try Harder" company. It is also one of the largest employee-owned firms in the United States, as you may remember from one of their advertising slogans: "At Avis, our employees are acting like they own the place."

In 1946 Warren Avis, a U.S. Air Force officer believed that airlines would soon become the primary mode of transportation throughout the country, so he decided to rent cars at airports. He opened the country's first airport car rental counters in Detroit and Miami. By 1948 he had opened locations in downtown areas as well as airports, and by 1954 there were 185 Avis locations in the U.S., ten in Canada, one in Mexico, and working agreements with local car companies overseas in seven countries. Avis sold the company in 1954 for $8 million, and since then Avis, Inc., has been controlled by twelve owners, including Avis.

The last owner in 1986 was a company called Wesray. CEO and chairman Joseph Vittoria was there at the time and learned that Wesray was willing to sell the firm to the employees. So with Vittoria leading the way, the employees bought the firm through an ESOP—employee stock ownership plan—for $1.75 billion on September 25, 1987. They kept 15 percent of the stock for top managers and the remaining 85 percent for other employees.

The employee-owners took action immediately to inject some democracy into the way they ran their company. They inaugurated employee participation groups (EPGs), which meet every month at all of their field locations. Each group of employees in a category *elects* a representative for a one-year term. They are the quality leaders. The quality leaders then elect representatives to attend quarterly zone meetings, the semiannual regional meetings, and the annual EPG national meeting held at world headquarters in Garden City, Long Island.

"Avis always thought 'We Try Harder' was the first simple mission statement," says Russell James, vice president in charge of quality for Avis, and a thirty-year employee. He says that in 1962 Chairman Robert Townsend used the phrase in a talk to the employees. It then became the backbone of their advertising campaigns, and the company's mission statement until 1990, when they started applying for the Malcolm Baldrige Award. They decided they needed a more detailed mission statement. Vittoria refused to write it. "He believed," recalled James, "that the mission statement had to be written by the one hundred and fifty employee groups—by area, department, and city. Let them write it and let it cascade up," recalls James. So that's what happened. One hundred and fifty mission statements rolled into headquarters.

Vittoria read them all, and then, four months later, wrote the corporate *Quest for Excellence*, reproduced here. The employee-owner representatives got a chance to review the document for final approval, and they made quite a few changes. One change, for example, was the word *profitability*. The employee-owners wanted it changed to **employee equity,** and it was.

The Avis Quest for Excellence is only one of the three documents that comprise Avis's mission statement. It is a guide for immediate actions and day-to-day decision making. "It's the game plan," says James. "It's what the 13,000 employee-owners get involved in." The other two documents are broader and help to set the goals and priorities that will take the company where it wants to go in the future. The *Value Statements* are designed to help each employee see how each of the visions relates to day-to-day experience. The *Vision Statement* is a concise list of the three areas in which Avis will always excel: customer service and satisfaction, employee participation, and return to shareholders.

Beyond this, Avis puts together a strategic plan book every year, which includes all 150 mission statements from the EPGs along with the corporate statements. *The Quest for Excellence, Vision Statement,* and *Value Statements* are updated whenever consensus demands it.

Employees at Avis appear happy. Empowerment is handled in an organized fashion, and employees solve customer complaints at the front-line level. But they are aware of their boundaries as well, and the system works. The number of complimentary letters to Avis always exceeds the complaint letters. After all, "total customer satisfaction" is in the first sentence of their mission statement.

Barrick

A World Class Mine
Operating Philosophy

Barrick Goldstrike Mines is dedicated to maintaining its position as a profitable organization and a leader in the mining industry.

In this way, we provide our shareholders a solid return on their investment, our employees with the benefits of gainful employment, and the surrounding community with a share in our prosperity.

Barrick has great respect for the environment and is committed to the protection of our natural resources for future generations.

It is our goal to work safely and efficiently at all times, thereby minimizing personal injuries, property damage, and other forms of loss. To this end, employee training and educational programs are integrated into our operations to ensure effective job performance and to foster long-term career development.

Barrick is committed to the aggressive pursuit of technological advancements for the purpose of improving operational efficiency and increasing profitability.

Success is achieved through teamwork. Activities are organized in a way that encourages our employees to work together. It is through our combined efforts that Barrick Goldstrike will maintain its position of leadership and profitability as "A World Class Mine."

Robert M. Smith
President and Chief Operating Officer

John O. McDonough
General Manager

An Example of a First Mission Statement

Our first corporate objective was to become a leading North American gold producer and to invest exclusively in North American properties.

Our second was to achieve growth through the acquisition and development of existing mines. The acquisition phase of our early years has evolved into the subsequent development of those properties, but we are always alert to opportunities for new acquisitions.

Our third was to follow conservative financial policies, maintaining a strong balance sheet that is not exposed to the risks of the financial markets.

Our fourth objective was to eliminate the risk of short-term fluctuations in the gold price with an effective hedging program. The result is that we are not only protected when prices fall, but also benefit from the upside potential when prices rise. This conservative financial approach is the necessary complement to our aggressive business style; together they build our long-term success.

Putting safety and security first in a risky business.

After being in the lackluster oil and gas business in the 1980s, American Barrick Resources chairman Peter Munk decided to go for the gold. In 1987 he purchased the Goldstrike Mine from Western States Minerals in Nevada for $62 million. Goldstrike was located in the so-called Carlin Trend, the richest vein of gold outside of South Africa.

At first the mine was thought to hold proven gold reserves of 600,000 ounces. However, later it was found to contain about 25 million ounces worth about $10 billion.

Clearly, Munk had made a smart purchase.

However, after looking around at other mining companies, Munk realized that there was one major flaw in the gold-mining business. When the price of the gold went down, company profits followed. Munk, a very conservative man, decided that to attract investors and shareholders he would have to solve this problem.

He announced his intention in the company's first mission statement, which had as its fourth objective: . . . **to eliminate the risk of short-term fluctuations in the gold price with an effective hedging program.** Simply put, Barrick uses a sophisticated and extensive commodity-hedging policy that has become a role model for other mining companies to follow.

This conservative approach to mining was very different from what other companies were doing when Munk took over the Toronto-based Barrick. Prior to Munk's arrival on the scene, gold miners often thought of themselves as gamblers and wildcatters just hoping to hit that big strike and then go into town and whoop it up. While hedging is now standard procedure with almost all mining companies, none does it to the extent of Barrick. These competitors don't always hedge, because when the gold price skyrockets, they want to take full advantage of the upside swing. On the other hand, when prices drop they hurt deeply. Most mining companies run fiscally responsible operations, but the gambling mentality still exists.

"Munk saw gold as insurance," says Greg Wilkins, the company's executive director, office of the chairman. "With changes occurring all over the world, including political unrest in South Africa [the world's largest gold producer], our philosophy has always been to use hedge products."

Wilkins says that the company's mission statement has been fine-tuned since 1983 to deal with the changing circumstances of the day.

For example, the first mission statement called for the company to **invest exclusively in North American properties.** "We've had to modify that," says Wilkins. "We're expanding into Latin America and looking at opportunities in China."

Wilkins also says that the company's current mission statement, now called the *Operating Philosophy*, takes into account the new realities of worker safety. Mining has long been considered one of the most dangerous jobs in the world, and it's an issue that is directly addressed in the *Operating Philosophy*: **It is our goal to work safely and efficiently at all times, thereby minimizing personal injuries, property damage, and other forms of loss.**

"We don't think any amount of gold is worth the cost of human life. Everything we do safeguards life, property, and the environment," says Wilkins, who adds that there's an economic side to this issue too. "It costs incredible amounts of money even for simple injuries. We try to implant in people's minds an attitude that safety is crucial, and you can't instill that attitude unless you make it part of your mission statement."

As far as property damage is concerned, mining equipment is large and expensive and everyone benefits when the gear is taken care of by workers, adds Wilkins. That's why minimizing property damage is singled out as well.

The mission statement also calls on the company to provide shareholders with a solid return on investment and the employees with the benefits of gainful employment. Profits have climbed 70 percent and the stock price soared 71 percent in 1993. By any measure, Barrick is perhaps the most successful mining operation around. Top executives make about 10 percent less than their counterparts at other companies but can make millions on stock options if the company prospers. The miners themselves can increase their average $40,000-a-year salaries an additional 10 percent if they meet quotas.

The company uses technology to keep costs in check. The mission statement calls for the **aggressive pursuit of technological advances for the purpose of improving operational efficiency and increasing profitability.** To this end, Barrick claims to have the most sophisticated autoclaves in the industry. (Autoclaves help separate gold from other material.)

Obviously, the biggest issue facing mining today is the environment. Although many staunch environmentalists don't believe any mining at all should be allowed, Barrick believes that it can be environmentally responsible and still run efficiently and profitably. **Barrick has great respect for the environment and is committed to the protection of our natural resources for future generations.**

"Clearly we don't want to dump a mine in the middle of Yellowstone National Park," says Wilkins, "but we believe we can conduct operations for the benefit of our shareholders, employees, and neighbors and contribute to the overall economy without interfering with what people want to do with the public lands."

Some detractors say this is just double-talk for "who cares what happens to some desolate areas in Nevada, where nobody wants to live anyway," but Goldstrike's approach is vastly different from many mining companies when it responds to critics. Instead of hunkering down and being defensive, the company becomes proactive. "We stand up and invite our critics to visit our mining operation, to see for themselves. Many environmental groups don't want to admit that we're running a pretty good operation," says Wilkins. "Our operating philosophy pertaining to the environment has been key in this fight. When critics attack us, we stand up and invite them to see what we're doing. We don't have to scramble like other companies."

Ben & Jerry's

Ben & Jerry's is dedicated to the creation and demonstration of a new corporate concept of linked prosperity. Our mission consists of three interrelated parts:

PRODUCT MISSION: To make, distribute, and sell the finest quality, all-natural ice cream and related products in a wide variety of innovative flavors made from Vermont dairy products.

SOCIAL MISSION: To operate the company in a way that actively recognizes the central role that business plays in the structure of society by initiating innovative ways to improve the quality of life of a broad community—local, national and international.

ECONOMIC MISSION: To operate the company on a sound financial basis of profitable growth, increasing value for our shareholders, and creating career opportunities and financial rewards for our employees.

Underlying the mission of Ben & Jerry's is the determination to seek new and creative ways of addressing all three parts, while holding a deep respect for the individuals, inside and outside the company, and for the communities of which they are a part.

A mission statement that encourages tension.

Tension wouldn't usually be the first thing to come to mind when thinking about ice cream, but at Ben & Jerry's tension is what their mission statement is all about.

Ben & Jerry's is dedicated to the creation and demonstration of a new corporate concept of linked prosperity. This means that all three parts of the mission statement—product mission, social mission, and economic mission—must be addressed simultaneously. Ben & Jerry's will not make a corporate decision that furthers one at the expense of the others.

Paradoxically, this tension actually makes daily life *less* stressful at the ice cream maker. "Since we developed our mission statement, decisions are much easier," says Henry Morgan, a director of Ben & Jerry's and the author, in 1989, of their mission statement. "Most mission statements are useless if they are single-focused," he says. "The reality is that business has multiple objectives. That's why I wrote Ben & Jerry's with three missions—product, economic, and social."

Morgan is no stranger to mission statements. He serves on twenty boards of directors, was the head of personnel for Polaroid, and also was the dean of the business school at Boston University. He knew about tension and made sure Ben & Jerry's mission statement included it.

A few years ago milk prices dropped below what was viable for Vermont farmers. Looking at all the ramifications, Ben & Jerry's decided to pay more than the asking price for milk and support their local farmers rather than go out of state or pay them the going rate. Why? If Ben & Jerry's bought milk from farmers in other states, it would violate their product mission to use milk . . . **made from Vermont dairy products.** On the other hand, if the Vermont farmers received only the going rate, they might lose their farms and that would violate Ben & Jerry's social mission . . . **to improve the quality of life of a broad community—local, national and international.** So they kept their missions intact by paying above the asking price. They didn't violate their economic mission statement because they still made a profit.

Another recent example of sticking to their mission statement—and balancing the parts as well—was the issue of bovine growth hormone. The bovine growth hormone occurs naturally in dairy cows, but the genetically engineered form, known as rBGH or RBST, is being marketed to dairy farmers to increase milk production. Ben & Jerry's customers have told them that they do not want products from rBGH-treated cows. Their dairy supplier, the Saint Albans Cooperative, maintains a policy that it will not accept milk from rBGH-treated cows, but Ben & Jerry's pays a premium to the Saint Albans Cooperative farmers in exchange for their reassurance that they will not use rBGH. Ben & Jerry's certainly could buy cheaper milk from farmers who used rBGH, but their mission statements prevent them from doing so. So they compromise, being true to the **all-natural** part of the product mission and the social mission of **improving the quality of life of a broad community** (in other words, keeping them in business). Again, they still made a profit.

The mission statement also calls for the company to . . . **seek new and creative ways of addressing all three parts** . . . So far, it seems to be working.

Ben & Jerry's have been making ice cream for ten years. Ben & Jerry were seventh-graders together on Long Island, New York. In 1977 they moved to Vermont and took a $5 correspondence course in ice cream–making from Penn State (yes, really!). A year later, with a $12,000 investment, Ben and Jerry opened their first ice cream scoop shop in a renovated gas station in Burlington, Vermont. In 1980 they decided to pack their ice cream in pints and try to get grocery store distribution in addition to the restaurants they serviced. By 1981 *Time* in an article about the new boom in ice cream, called Ben & Jerry's "the best ice cream in the world." By 1984, with its distribution channels widened, franchises opened, and a public stock offering made, Ben and Jerry's sales exceeded $4 million, a 120 percent increase from 1983. In 1987 Ben & Jerry's introduced their first "living" flavor—Cherry Garcia, named for the Grateful Dead guitarist Jerry Garcia. In 1993 they added their second "living" flavor—Wavy Gravy ice cream, in honor of the counterculture hero. By 1992 total sales were $132 million.

In keeping with their economic mission, **To operate the company on a sound financial basis** . . . Ben & Jerry's had a corporate salary policy that was unique to the United States. The compressed compensation ratio said that the company's highest paid employee—including management—could not earn more than seven times what the lowest paid full-time regular employee earned. However, in mid-1994, when Ben Cohen stepped down as CEO, he and Jerry Greenfield decided they needed to change this pay cap in order to attract a more mainstream pool of candidates to the top job. The company was now a $140 million concern and they both believed that more traditional management was necessary. The two founders decided not to abandon all of their idiosyncracies though. They opened the list of potential CEOs to anyone willing to write an essay on why they should be CEO of Ben & Jerry's.

BINNEY & SMITH

CORPORATE VALUES
The character and nature of our company. The behaviors we expect everyone to follow and reinforce with each other regardless of position or level.

BUSINESS OBJECTIVE
What we want to achieve: Profitable revenue growth through Continuous Improvement by involvement of all employees.

BUSINESS OPERATING PRINCIPLES
The business principles that guide the decision making actions of our people.

BUSINESS MISSION
The business we're in: The best quality, safest products for colorful visual expression for enjoyment, learning and work.

THE CONTINUOUS IMPROVEMENT
V·I·S·I·O·N

Individuals and groups of motivated and innovative people willing to listen, who work together to solve problems and improve processes, in a supportive and progressive environment which encourages and welcomes change.

HOW THE CONTINUOUS IMPROVEMENT PROCESS WORKS

The 5 ways of working together that enable us to achieve our business and personal goals:

Focus on the customer to provide great service.

Flatter organization structure to eliminate bureaucracy.

Faster decision making to speed up results.

Flexible actions and reactions to consumer and customer needs.

Fun and profit, which go together.

HOW CONTINUOUS IMPROVEMENT MEETS INDIVIDUAL NEEDS

* Provide training to enable people to be involved and creative in problem solving.

* Encourage individuals and groups to take greater responsibility and make their own decisions.

* Recognize people for changing things for the better.

* Improve communications and mutual respect.

* Promote leadership and a sense of security.

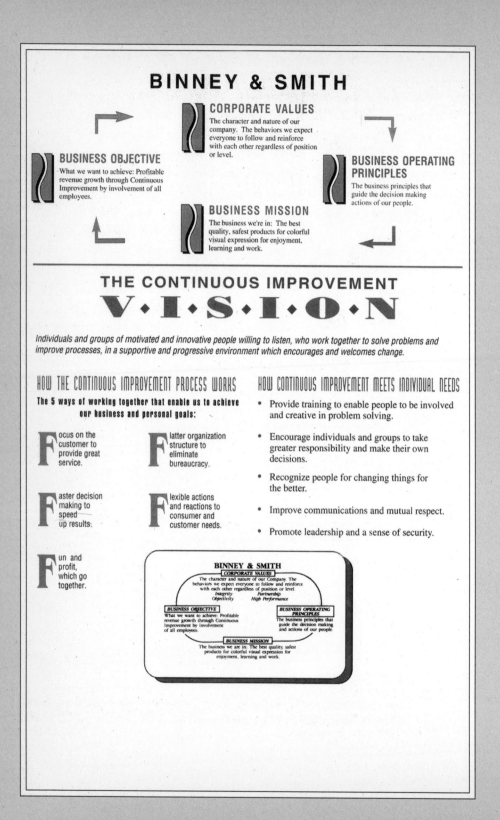

BINNEY & SMITH

CORPORATE VALUES
The character and nature of our Company. The behaviors we expect everyone to follow and reinforce with each other regardless of position or level.
Integrity   Partnership
Objectivity   High Performance

BUSINESS OBJECTIVE
What we want to achieve: Profitable revenue growth through Continuous Improvement by involvement of all employees.

BUSINESS OPERATING PRINCIPLES
The business principles that guide the decision making and actions of our people.

BUSINESS MISSION
The business we are in: The best quality, safest products for colorful visual expression for enjoyment, learning and work.

Business Operating Principles

- Satisfy important, lasting consumer needs by producing and marketing high quality, branded products.

- Provide superior performing, innovatively designed products with high perceived value at fair consumer prices.

- Maintain share leadership of each core product category in which we compete via aggressive and innovative marketing support for our brands.

- Develop new product lines and businesses that offer substantial opportunity for long-term growth.

- Earn high profit margins by being a large volume producer of products, at the lowest possible total cost.

- Provide a working environment where employees are treated equitably as individuals and enjoy a sense of security.

- Be a responsible corporate citizen.

- Provide a fair, consistent rate of return to the shareholder.

Corporate Values

These are the character and nature of our company that we expect everyone to follow and reinforce with each other regardless of position or level.

Integrity

- Conduct yourself with the highest standards of ethics, personally and corporately.
- Conduct honest, open, and forthright dealings inside and outside the company.
- Conduct fair and equitable treatment of employees, customers, suppliers and the community.
- Conduct yourself and your organization in a fiscally moderate way.

Objectivity

- Make a clear-eyed assessment of facts in a candid way.
- Face up to difficult issues and act in a timely, appropriate manner.
- Speak up freely and openly without fear.

Partnership

- Work with others to achieve mutual, compatible business goals.
- Trust others to say what they mean and to do what they say they will.
- Seek collaboration from others to engender broad-based support for your efforts.
- Provide a secure workplace for our employees.

High Performance

- Produce above-average sales and profit growth over time by consistent execution of our business strategies.
- Outperform competition through creativity and innovation rather than spending.
- Maintain high quality products through consumer sensitivity and stringent quality control procedures.
- Achieve above-average productivity in manufacturing systems and operations, and administrative and organizational effectiveness.

BINNEY & SMITH ®

Color it circular.

Binney & Smith, makers of Crayola crayons, Magic Markers, Silly Putty, and Liquitex paints, are in business to make "the best quality, safest products for colorful visual expression for enjoyment, learning and work." They call their mission statement the *Business Model* and it contains four interdependent elements: *Corporate Values*, *Business Operating Principles*, *Business Mission*, and *Business Objective*.

The *Business Mission* and the *Business Objective* are the simplest and most concise elements of the *Business Model* because they summarize the overall business goals of Binney & Smith: to achieve financial success by producing high-quality artists' materials. The steps to getting there—the values and the principles—are more complex and are expanded upon in great detail in additional handouts. "It's a complete circle," says Eric Zebley, internal communications manager. "All four areas are equally important, and all are part of what Binney & Smith is about."

There are seven business operating principles, beginning with consumer needs and ending with an obligation to shareholders. The *Values* are the principles Binney & Smith employees concentrate on to make sure they get the job done in the best possible way and achieve their *Mission* and *Objective*.

When *Corporate Values* were put in writing in 1988, *The Rainbow Reporter*, Binney & Smith's internal communications vehicle, did an article to introduce it to all their employees worldwide. Enclosed in each copy of the newsletter was a wallet-size laminated card with the *Business Model* on one side and the *Business Operating Principles* on the other.

"The *Business Mission* has been refined since 1988, to reflect changes in product lines and strategies. The one you see was done in 1992," Zebley says. One big change in their *Business Mission* concerned the toy market. "We used to be involved in the toy business and our *Business Mission* at the time addressed that. We tried to put our name on a lot of products—flash cards and other things like that," says Zebley. "But we discovered it wasn't the business we should be in. That's when we came up with a really strong business statement." **The business we're in: the best quality, safest products for colorful visual expression for enjoyment, learning and work.** "We found that this area [toys] didn't meet our *Business Objective*," he says. But wait a minute—what about Silly Putty? "Silly Putty is the exception," says Zebley. "It is a toy-oriented product, but it is a visual expression," he says. "Silly Putty turned forty in 1990, and we introduced four new colors and revitalized the line. At special holidays we add different colors, pastels for Easter, green and red at Christmas, and orange at Halloween."

"The *Values* statement is framed and hung in all our facilities," says Zebley. "We are trying to make employees aware of the values. Even when employees are evaluated, they will be judged against the *Values*." Even the disciplinary policy has been affected by the *Values* statements. "In the past, our disciplinary policy was rather abrupt, not proactive," Zebley adds. They've even changed the name from **disciplinary policy** to **conduct of performance expectations.** "We are incorporating the values as part of this policy now. For example, an employee works in the crayon department. He comes to work on time and meets all his quotas, but he doesn't get along with people. Before, it was hard to address that in accordance with our disciplinary policy. But now we take a different approach, and quote the *Values* statement under the partnership section about getting along with others." **Work with others to achieve mutual, compatible business goals.** "We would work with that employee to improve in that area," he says.

When job interviews are done at the plants, the perspective employees are asked how to exhibit the four values: **Integrity, Objectivity, Partnership,** and **High Performance.** "Candidate selection for positions at Binney & Smith include a section on *their* values as well," says Zebley. It is stated on their interview evaluation form: "When interviewing candidates for positions at Binney & Smith, it is imperative that we include not only their qualifications based on specifications for the position, but emphasize their demonstrated behaviors and accomplishments that are consistent with the *Corporate Values*. This form is meant as a guide to evaluating these values and must be completed by each interviewer for all candidates. Be sure to list specific evidence to reflect their accomplishments and/or behaviors to substantiate their commitment to or lack of commitment to these *Corporate Values*."

The corporate value of **High Performance** is a critical one to the company's success, and creativity is addressed here. **Outperform competition through creativity and innovation rather than spending.** "High performance means outperforming the competition," says Zebley. "We are in the art and stationery business for children and adults. Creativity helps us to be different, on the cutting edge. Fun is an important part of our company as well. We want our product and programs to be fun, developmental, colorful, and to allow children and adults to be able to express themselves. If you're not creative yourself, how can you expect the people that you create products for to be creative? Some companies will hire outside creative people to come up with creative solutions to a problem, but we bring in our own people from different areas of the company," he says. Fun is so important to Binney & Smith that they do what very few other companies dare to do: They include the word *fun* in their mission statement. Look in the *The Continuous Improvement* section and you will find: **Fun and profit, which go together.**

Binney & Smith continues to use their weekly newsletter, to educate employees about their corporate values. "In May [1994]," says Zebley, "we'll start a four-part series on the *Corporate Values*, highlighting each one with an example of a person or a department. And our summer edition of the *Rainbow Reporter* will also feature the *Corporate Values*."

The Binney & Smith business model, with its four elements, has been further refined to include their *Continuous Improvement Vision*, which is employee focused and revolves around teamwork and empowerment. "We feel employees have the answers to a lot of things we need to know," says Zebley. "We've empowered employees to make decisions. Our plants are organized into work teams. These individuals do maintenance, scheduling, order their own products and their own raw materials. It helps them take more [pride of] ownership into the company. Five years ago, we had a quality assurance department. If a molder ran a crayon color, a Q.A. person would come out and test the match. Now the employee does the quality check themselves right on the line, which is a direct result of the corporate values of **High Performance, Objectivity,** and **Partnership**," he says.

Today, Binney & Smith makes more than two billion crayons and more than two hundred million markers every year. Headquartered in Easton, Pennsylvania, Binney & Smith has manufacturing facilities in the U.S., England, and Mexico City and distribution centers all over the world. Their products are sold in more than eighty countries. Binney & Smith has been owned by Hallmark Cards since 1984.

Binney & Smith reportedly has the lion's share of the U.S. crayon market but won't reveal the figures. They also are more expensive than most other brands. "Our crayons might cost a little more because we create a better, innovative product," says Zebley.

We couldn't resist telling you these fun facts about Binney & Smith products.

- On an average, children between the ages of two and seven color 28 minutes daily.
- Binney & Smith makes over six million Silly Putty eggs each year.
- The average child in the U.S. will wear down 730 crayons by his or her tenth birthday.
- The scent of Crayola crayons is among the 20 most recognizable to American adults.
- The Crayola color called flesh was renamed peach in 1962, partly as a result of the civil rights movement.
- The Crayola brand is recognized by 99 percent of Americans.
- Crayola boxes are printed in 11 languages.
- Astronauts during NASA's Apollo 8 mission used Silly Putty to fasten down tools during weightlessness.

Boeing

Corporate Direction

LONG-RANGE MISSION

To be the number one aerospace company in the world and among the premier industrial concerns in terms of quality, profitability, and growth.

FUNDAMENTAL GOALS

- **Quality** as measured by: customer, employee, and community satisfaction.
- **Profitability** as measured against our ability to achieve and then maintain: 20 percent average annual return on stockholders' equity.
- **Growth** over the plan period as measured against a goal to achieve: Greater than 5 percent average annual real sales growth from 1988 base.

OBJECTIVES

To achieve the above goals and fulfill the Boeing mission, the following objectives will guide company actions:

- **Continuous improvement in quality of products and processes:** Our commitment to steady, long-term improvement in our products and processes is the cornerstone of our business strategy. To achieve this objective, we must work to continuously improve the overall efficiency and productivity of our design, manufacturing, administrative, and support organizations.

- ***A highly skilled and motivated workforce:***
  Our most important resource is our human resource: the people who design and build our products and service our customers. Given the right combination of skills, training, communication, environment, supervision, and technical support, we believe our employees will achieve the needed gains in productivity and quality to meet our goals.
- ***Capable and focused management:***
  To employ our technical and human resources with optimum efficiency, we must ensure that managers are carefully selected, appropriately trained, and work together to achieve our long-range goals.
- ***Technical excellence:***
  In a world of fast-changing technology, we can only remain competitive by continuously refining and expanding our technical capability.
- ***Financial strength:***
  The high-risk cyclical nature of our business demands a strong financial base. We must retain the capital resources to meet our current commitments and make substantial investments to develop new products and new technology for the future.
- ***Commitment to integrity:***
  Integrity, in the broadest sense, must pervade our actions in all relationships, including those with our customers, suppliers, and each other. This is a commitment to uncompromising values and conduct. It includes compliance with all laws and regulations.

Integrity Statement

Integrity is a fundamental part of Boeing history and of the way we do business. Our commitment to integrity means that all of our actions and relationships are based on these uncompromising values:

Treat each other with respect

•

Deal fairly in all of our relationships

•

Honor our commitments and obligations

- Communicate honestly

- Take responsibility for our actions

- Deliver safe and reliable products of the highest quality

- Provide equal opportunity to all

- Comply with all laws and regulations

Boeing Management Attributes

APPENDIX TO CORPORATE POLICY 8D10, ADDENDUM A

Boeing will evaluate, promote, and retain managers on the basis of the following attributes:

- Has a record of excellent performance with the highest ethical standards
- Is committed to The Boeing Company, its principles, objectives, and goals
- Leads Continuous Quality Improvement focused on Customer satisfaction
- Treats people with fairness, trust, and respect
- Removes barriers, promotes teamwork, and empowers people to improve business performance
- Demonstrates innovation and seeks to improve technical and business competence
- Seeks intellectual growth and learning
- Coaches people to develop their capabilities
- Shares information, listens to others, and maintains objectivity
- Provides timely communication on results and processes

The target numbers are tough; the ethics are tougher.

It all came together in 1988. "From 1984 on, there were sporadic efforts on quality, you know the Jurans and Demings," says Art Carter, Jr., Boeing's vice president of continuous quality improvement. "We did some work in organizational behavior and focusing of our goals. We felt it was time to get it all together under one umbrella. That's when we wrote the *Corporate Direction*."

There have been no changes in the *Direction* since its inception in 1988 even though it is reviewed regularly. "We review it every six months" says Carter, "every spring and fall. We want to make sure: do we still believe it, is it right for us? It's a living document. It's not cast in stone."

The items that always come up for sharp discussion, however, are the target figures: **Profitability as measured against our ability to achieve and then maintain: 20 percent average annual return on stockholders' equity.** Says Carter: "There's always concern that the return on equity is a little high, but we decided to leave it alone. Clearly, it's a stretch goal. It's a shot for us, a long shot. We're in a cyclical business."

Growth over the plan period as measured against a goal to achieve: Greater than 5 percent average real sales growth from 1988 base. "We're always thinking about changing that five-percent figure. But what would we change it to? It's one of the things we look at all the time. We tend to think that you have to step up to the bar and say what you want. If it's to stretch a goal so be it," Carter says. "You know if we grew five percent every year from now until 2000 we'd probably have to buy one hundred companies of the Fortune 500 to do it."

Interestingly, the *Direction* talks about how to handle financial dangers unique to the aircraft industry: **The high-risk cyclical nature of our business demands a strong financial base. We must retain the capital resources to meet our current commitments and make sub-**

stantial investments to develop new products and new technology for the future. In 1993, Boeing spent $1.66 billion—more than 15 percent of its revenue—on research and development. On the plus side, NASA has chosen Boeing as the prime contractor for the $20-plus-billion space station project.

Currently, Boeing and other aircraft makers are being hit with a one-two punch. The commercial airline business is in its own slump while some defense-related contracts are shrinking with the end of the Cold War. Fortunately, the company has lowered its dependence on defense work in anticipation of the ending of the Cold War. This type of work will probably never return. Boeing is also in a strong position to capitalize on the next commercial airline expansion, as it has garnered 60 percent of the commercial airplane business. Its 777 jet, which is entering commercial service in 1995, will compete directly against the Airbus 330 built by European consortium Airbus Industrie.

"We've taken on some debt but we're in a strong cash position to weather the cycle. Generally, the cycles have been somewhat offset by each other—defense/space and commercial—but ever since we declared peace, our defense/space business has gone in the toilet," says Carter.

Mainly because of its government contracts, Boeing's leadership decided there was no room for even a whisper of dishonesty among anyone at the company. **Integrity, in the broadest sense, must pervade our actions in all relationships, including those with our customers, suppliers, and each other. This is a commitment to uncompromising values and conduct. It includes compliance with all laws and regulations.** But isn't complying with all laws and regulations a given? "You can say it's a given," notes Carter, "but it's nice to really say it. We look at integrity issues especially as it affects our government contracts. We chose to just come down squeaky clean with no gray areas."

Still another section of the *Corporate Direction* was broken out. The section about having a **Capable and focused management: . . . we must ensure that managers are carefully selected, appropriately trained, and work together to achieve our long-range goals.** In 1988, the company issued a set of *Desired Management Attributes*. However, in 1993, these attributes were reexamined by Chairman Frank Shrontz and President Phil Condit prompted by employee complaints that management was not, as they put it in a companywide letter, "walking the talk." Shrontz and Condit wrote: "While definitely not a general condition across Boeing management, the actions perceived are enough to undermine our credibility and employees' commitment concerning our improvement objectives."

They decided to delete the word *Desired* from the title. In other words, these are the management attributes that are now mandatory, not simply desired. Moreover, they also added some teeth to the attributes in that the company was now going to evaluate, promote, and retain managers on the basis of how they follow these attributes. "It may sound a little folksy," says Carter, "but the CEO and president made them up. We owed it to our managers to tell them the kind of attributes we wanted to see in our preferred future, and we won't get there until we reward and promote these behaviors. We haven't always done that in the past. In the past, we've rewarded people based on their functional skills and capabilities, and cared about their ability to lead later on. We now have a list of the attributes we want to reward, promote, and underpin with compensation." What if a manager still isn't getting it? "Both Frank and Phil believe you have the obligation to retrain people, help them and give them time to change. You must give them the opportunity to retrain or change the way they manage," says Carter.

And how does the company know when a manager is meeting the attributes? "Every manager mails out a questionnaire to superiors, peers, and subordinates to survey these people about how well the manager adheres to these attributes," says Carter. "Data is collected by a third party and provided to the manager. We've just started with this program; it's our first year. In fact, we started with the CEO."

Boston Beer Company

Company Philosophy

We are the Boston Beer Company.

We make the Best Beer in America.

We treat others as we would like to be treated ourselves.

We sell our beer with enthusiasm, energy for our jobs and respect for our customers.

As a company, we seek to add value to our customers, by providing them with a superior product at a favorable price; to our employees, by providing them with employment which encourages personal growth and pride at favorable compensations; to our investors, by providing a superior return on their investment; and to our communities, by providing taxes, charitable contributions, and community support.

Because we represent the Company at all times, we act in a manner which increases the respect of others for the Boston Beer Company and its people.

We constantly seek ways to improve our own skills and how we do our jobs.

We are committed to making Samuel Adams the largest and most respected craft or imported beer in the United States before 2006.

A timetable for action.

"I started the company," says Jim Koch (pronounced "cook"), owner of the Boston Beer Company, "and was able to build it according to my vision as to how a great company would treat itself." Koch wrote the corporate mission statement, the *Company Philosophy* himself and every sentence includes the word *we* on purpose.

We are the Boston Beer Company. Why state the obvious? "People in a company get 'they' disease," says Koch. "People say 'I wonder when *they're* going to do this, I wonder when *they're* going to do that.' What I wanted to communicate is that there is no 'they,' it's 'we.' We decide what we're going to do. Everybody who joins the Boston Beer Company is part of it. There's no third party here. It surprises people when I say companies don't exist. There is no such thing as a company. Have you seen one? Touched it? They're purely a legal construct. Go into the law books and you'll find that a corporation is a legal fiction. A company is a set of learned patterns of behaviors. People have learned to come to the Boston Beer Company to do a certain thing; customers have learned that if they see Samuel Adams on the bottle, it's going to taste a certain way. Our suppliers know that we prefer certain kinds of malt and hops. To the extent there's a company, it's simply a way people have changed their behavior to accommodate a certain goal," he says passionately.

We make the Best Beer in America. Pretty heady words. Jim Koch brews Samuel Adams beer with a recipe created by his great-great-grandfather Louis Koch 131 years ago. He is the sixth oldest son in a row to be a brewmaster. "We had actually won a number of awards from the Association of Brewers for being the best beer, so it was already a reality when I wrote it," says Koch.

Sell[ing] our beer with enthusiasm relates directly to the employees. "We go through a lot before we hire somebody," he says. "We look for people who have a list of characteristics; in sales we look for people who are proactive, discerners, good strategists, good persuaders, and have an achievement orientation. We work very hard to make sure when we hire somebody that we set them up to succeed. We make sure the requirements of the job match the behavior that they feel comfortable with, and the needs that motivate them. We have to look at their best interests and sometimes it's not in their best interests to put them in a job where they could fail. As a result, our turnover rate is around five percent. We haven't lost a person in the office or brewery in five years," he says. "In fact, we've been trying to find someone for Phoenix for over a year and we've been through two thousand résumés and haven't hired anyone yet."

An employee's first day at the Boston Beer Company is a little different from at other companies. "I meet with everybody on their first day of orientation and taste beer with them," says Koch. "I point out the characteristics of Samuel Adams that make it the best beer in America."

The longest paragraph in the *Company Philosophy* is about adding value in a number of different ways: . . . **we seek to add value to our customers, by providing them with a superior product at a favorable price** . . . If you've heard their radio commercials, which Koch voices himself, he talks about noble hops, which he claims are the rarest in the world. Noble hops can cost up to twenty times as much as other, coarser hops and they can be grown only in three small valleys in middle Europe.

. . . **superior product at a favorable price** . . . Despite the high price of noble hops, Koch endeavors to keep the price reasonable. "We've raised our price only once in ten years," he says, "and that was when the government increased the excise tax. That's our way of giving back to the consumers. We also make a cranberry beer in the winter and we literally lose money on it. We don't make a lot of it, but it's good for Christmas presents. We charge the same as we do for Sam Adams."

. . . **charitable contributions, and community support** play a big role at the Boston Beer Company, starting with their brewery. "We located our brewery in an old brewery that was a community development project. We were the lead tenant on renovating this old brewery in Boston's Jamaica Plain neighborhood in 1984," says Koch. "The brewery is owned by the neighborhood development corporation. The objective of renovating the brewery was to provide jobs for the neighborhood and stabilize the neighborhood. It's been successful at doing that," he says. The Boys and Girls Club of Boston is their main benefactor. "We run tours for about thirty thousand people a year," says Koch. "Everyone is asked to contribute a dollar for the tour and that goes to the Boys and Girls Club. We literally contribute to hundreds of events around the country by providing our product to charities at wholesale prices," says Koch. Another benefactor was President Clinton. When Koch learned that Samuel Adams Lager was the beer of choice for then President-elect Clinton, he was thrilled and decided to donate Samuel Adams beer to all ten inaugural balls and dinners.

Because we represent the Company at all times, we act in a manner which increases the respect of others for the Boston Beer Company and its people is a critical point in this philosophy, says Koch. "This closes the circle with the first statement that 'we' are the company. The impression we leave on people is their impression of the Boston Beer Company. This sentence is a reminder for people to adhere to their best self. Employees can drink while representing the company, but they're encouraged to drink responsibly and required not to do anything reckless or illegal. You can always take a cab home from a promotion and always take a cab back in the morning to get your car and no one will question it," he says. "There's no shame in it. It reflects good judgment."

. . . improve our own skills . . . is the next tenet. "We spend a lot of time and money on training," says Koch. "I believe you're either growing or dying. We promote from within; we push employees to get better. Our salespeople get from two to six weeks of formal sit-down training a year by outside professional trainers," he says.

The last statement in the philosophy looks toward the future—2006 to be exact. "It's nice to have a goal that is both visionary and concrete. That's a very specific measurable goal," says Koch. "We can measure our progress every year against that." But why **2006?** "My partner and I developed a plan when we started in 1984. We said twenty years after we got things rolling, which turned out to be 1986, we wanted to be the number-one beer in our category. Everyone who joins the company commits themselves personally to attaining that goal." He adds: "Above my desk is a little piece of paper with 2005 written on it. We want to match the biggest by 2005 and be the biggest by 2006. We plan against it and it helps me to think 'where am I going?' It's a map for me for the next twenty years. It enables me to do things with a very long perspective in mind. For the last ten years this has been our goal and we are ahead of our plan."

But what do the words **craft** beer mean? Koch explains: "Craft beer is an American beer that is made in the historical style with a lot of flavor and taste. It's a high-end American beer, but not a Bud. We're not going to pass Bud or Coors, but we can pass Heineken or Beck's. The customer thinks of domestic beers and imported beers and now there's this new category that we've spearheaded at microbreweries called hand-crafted beer."

Koch is so fervent about freshness that he would rather swim in his outdated beer than sell it and does, traditionally, every summer.

Leo Burnett

Our Corporate Mission

The mission of the Leo Burnett Company is to create superior advertising.

In Leo's words: "Our primary function in life is to produce the best advertising in the world, bar none.

"This is to be advertising so interrupting, so daring, so fresh, so engaging, so human, so believable and so well-focused as to themes and ideas that, at one and the same time, it builds a quality reputation for the long haul as it produces sales for the immediate present."

Operating Principles

PRODUCT: We recognize that the most important contribution we make to the success of our clients is Superior Advertising.

CLIENTS: We will work with a select group of clients who believe in advertising, whose businesses depend on Superior Advertising, who represent sizeable potential, who believe in partnership, and whose compensation policies and business ethics are compatible with our own.

PEOPLE: We will employ only talented, idea-oriented people with high standards, who love advertising, demonstrate respect for other people, exhibit a sense of competitive pride, display an eagerness to excel and who put their client's interest before their own.

ENVIRONMENT: We will maintain a climate, in terms of working conditions, human relations, opportunities for growth, self-expression, and monetary rewards, that will attract the best people and provide them with the most stimulating, rewarding and enjoyable career in the advertising business.

ORGANIZATION: We will organize and staff to achieve our Superior Advertising Mission for every client, in every office; and, by going beyond that, to make a broad and positive contribution to the client's entire, on-going marketing effort.

MARKETS: We will operate only in markets where current or potential clients exist, or will exist, in a major way. Our offices, in any market where we do business, must be capable of delivering Superior Advertising.

NEW BUSINESS: We will plan and pursue an aggressive new business program, recognizing that new clients, and new assignments from current clients, bring new challenges and opportunities, enhance our reputation, attract talented people, broaden our revenue base and contribute to the long-term health of the Agency. Since our primary responsibility is to current clients, new business should not take precedence over, nor get in the way of, those relationships.

REPUTATION: We will strive to be recognized as the best advertising agency in every market where we do business, based on our ability to produce Superior Advertising, to grow our client's business, to maintain enduring client relationships, to provide our people with the most stimulating and rewarding working environment and to conduct ourselves as responsible members of the communities where we do business.

FINANCIAL: We will be a privately-held company because that gives us the freedom to allocate our financial resources in the best interest of our clients and our people.

INTEGRITY: We will operate, at all times, in an ethical and moral manner, as if Leo were looking over our shoulders.

"In Leo's Words . . ."

What do the Green Giant, the Marlboro Man, Tony the Tiger, the Pillsbury Doughboy, the Keebler Elves, and the Good Hands at Allstate have in common? One thing. They were all created by the Leo Burnett Company.

The Leo Burnett Company is the largest single advertising agency in the U.S., with 6,400 employees. Single, because other agencies have merged to form giant conglomerates, but Leo Burnett stands alone—alone, with billings of $4.1 billion annually. The company is privately owned; all stockholders are active employees.

Leo Burnett's mission is interesting in that it actually quotes the founder. **In Leo's words** . . . "It's about producing superior advertising—nothing else," but in 1988 the executive committee felt they needed something more. Most members of the executive committee had worked with Leo Burnett. William T. Lynch, president and chief executive officer, had started with the company first as a trainee, then as an assistant account executive. Burnett's philosophies had always been passed down verbally, kind of like family folklore. The executive committee wanted to put it together and Lynch recalls that they gathered all the memos they could find (the pile was about five feet tall) and looked at the ones that wrestled with problems. A recurring theme of ten issues arose and the memos gave them ten principles that answered them. They took the exact quotes of memos from Burnett and other former management and compiled them into the *Operating Principles* used today. In fact, the last principle deals with integrity and reminds people to operate . . . **as if Leo were looking over our shoulders.**

Leo Burnett opened his Chicago advertising agency on August 5, 1935—right in the middle of the Great Depression. His office was small—five rooms—and he had eight associates. He also had three clients.

Today Burnett's client list is awesome. As a giant in the ad agency business you might think they have hundreds of accounts, but they don't. They try to keep the list around 35, but their clients include Allstate, the Beef Council, Fruit of the Loom, Hallmark, Heinz, Keebler, Kellogg's, Maytag, McDonald's, Oldsmobile, Phillip Morris, Pillsbury, Procter & Gamble, Reebok, Sony, StarKist, and United Air Lines. That's about half. Don't think new business isn't important to them. It's crucial. But their idea of new business is to grow with their current clients. **Since our primary responsibility is to current clients, new business should not take precedence over, nor get in the way of, those relationships.**

It seems to be working. Green Giant has retained Burnett since 1935, Phillip Morris since 1954, Oldsmobile since 1934, StarKist since 1958. The list goes on and the trend is almost unheard of in a business where an account goes up for agency review at the drop of a hat.

Burnett was a man of ideals. He had big dreams and wanted to achieve them. His spirit is still felt in everything the company does. Even now, in meetings, when discussions get heated, someone will say "what would Leo think" and the group reflects. The employees who work at Burnett still like to use the fat black Alpha pencils that Leo favored, and there is a little book called *The 100 Leos*, which are excerpts of his wit and wisdom.

The *Operating Principles* guide the Leo Burnett company internally, but their mission statement lights the way. Literally.

Lynch asks everyone to hang their copy of the mission statement right above their light switch. "That way, it's the last and first thing they see," says Lynch. "Leo tantalized us with a mission almost unattainable," says Lynch. "But I know he would be proud of us today—we just won the Smuckers account."

The Leo Burnett company is run on philosophies and symbols. The apple, which the company has been giving away to anyone who enters the office since 1935, is one of their symbols. Another symbol—a hand reaching for the stars—has been seen along with the company motto since 1938. In Burnett's words: "When you reach for the stars, you may not quite get one . . . but you won't come up with a handful of mud either." It symbolizes the company's constant striving for superior advertising. **Our primary function in life is to produce the best advertising in the world, bar none.**

Leo Burnett stepped down as chairman in 1967, and in his departure speech he offered words to work by and told employees that if they didn't hold true to these philosophies, he would insist they take his name off the door.

And, by golly, it will be taken off the door. Even if I have to materialize long enough some night to rub it out myself—on every one of your floors. And before I DE-materialize again, I will paint out that star-reaching symbol too. And burn all the stationery. Perhaps tear up a few ads in passing. And throw every goddamned apple down the elevator shafts. You just won't know the place the next morning. You'll have to find another name.

Campbell & Ferrara
Nurseries

Mission Statement

Campbell and Ferrara Nurseries, Inc., is a community-oriented garden center and landscape company.

Campbell and Ferrara strives to grow and sell top quality plants, and design and build gardens of beauty and value.

The **Campbell and Ferrara** family strives to provide the highest level of service and guaranteed total customer satisfaction.

Campbell and Ferrara strives to develop a knowledgeable and loyal staff of conscientious, career-minded people who are devoted to the enhancement of the horticultural field.

Campbell and Ferrara strives to profit through honesty, value and service.

Campbell and Ferrara Nurseries . . . *We have Nature To Share, Since 1945*

Providing continuity through the generations.

Campbell & Ferrara Nurseries is a one-location gardening and land-scaping center located in Alexandria, Virginia. It's been a family-owned business since its beginning in 1945. Campbell & Ferrara realized that they needed a mission statement in 1992, when they began to plan to transfer control of the business from the founders' generation to their children.

Jeff Minnich, senior vice president and second in command at Campbell & Ferrara, explains: "It was needed to set the stage for the next generation. It says this [the company] is ours and we're going to run it our way. This is the generation that's in control now, and we've said it with a positive statement to the whole company. This is what we stand for and we'll stand by it the best we can. It [our corporate mission statement] sent a strong message to the staff and the clientele saying that just because the old guys left, we're not dying. We're here," says Minnich.

Minnich is not part of the original nursery family, but his family and the Campbell and Ferrara clans go back several generations. "I'm not related to the families, but our families have known each other for three generations," he says. The elder Campbell left the business about five years ago. His partner, Ferrara, retired about two years ago. So the sons took over. Michael Ferrara decided to leave last year, and Minnich took his place, working his way up from his position as a landscape designer eleven years ago.

"We started a management training program a couple of years ago, in the summer of 1992," says Minnich. "We had a management consultant call us to suggest doing a swap job (a barter agreement). She said, 'I'd like my landscaping done and you guys are going through a generational change, so how about it?'

"So we got together with this management consultant and worked out a deal," says Minnich. "One of the first things she asked us was what our goals were. After forty-five years of mom-and-pop reactive management, we were taken aback. We'd never thought about it," says Minnich. "So we listed a series of goals, and she said, 'You should have a mission statement too. Something you can always go back to, to focus and direct you, and bring you back to earth.'

"So we had a meeting with all the landscape people and top management, about ten altogether, and started to put together this mission statement. What we wanted to put into our statement were the standard things like service and quality, but we wanted to take it a little further. We wanted employees to be happy, but learning, working hard and learning," he says.

"From 1945 to 1992 we didn't have a mission statement. Now we do, and it's truly amazing how it focuses you. Whenever we get really crazy and Jim [Campbell] has some wild, far-fetched idea, we'll pull it out and say, 'Does this satisfy this, does this satisfy that,' and we run through the *Mission Statement* and it really does help," he says.

The Campbell & Ferrara *Mission Statement* started out with their declaration of being **community-oriented**. "Jim and I are both in civic clubs and we're active on different boards," says Minnich. "There was a point a couple of months ago when I told Jim I was really overwhelmed; we had a lot of changes going on here and I said I wanted to get off some of these boards. He said I could do what I wanted, but what about our *Mission Statement*? So I'm staying on the boards."

Another area in which Campbell & Ferrara adheres to the community portion of their mission statement is with schools. "We host field trips from schools here and have school projects with gardens on the grounds of the nursery. We really started a lot of this up since the *Mission Statement*, especially right here in our own community."

One of the other things the *Mission Statement* helped them do was decide to focus on their landscape and garden center and sell the two growing farms they own in Maryland, which is covered in their third statement; . . . **strives to provide the highest level of service.** "We want to zero in right here," says Minnich. "We want to make the place more attractive, update the buildings, give the customer the best that we can possibly give. I don't think we're doing that right now," he says. "It's a goal. We need to improve service, staff, and the physical environment."

. . . **strives to profit through honesty, value and service** seems obvious, but they wanted to include it in the *Mission Statement.* "We've always done that, but having something in writing sort of ties you to an honor system," says Minnich. "You're more aware of it in the back of your mind. If we don't do it, we're falsely representing the company, and there are consequences."

One of the topics they may add to their next *Mission Statement* is environmental stewardship. Their philosophy about pesticides used to be if you saw an aphid, use a bug spray. Now they're suggesting alternative means to reducing bug populations and resorting to pesticides only when necessary for the plant's survival.

Campbell & Ferrara, for being just a one-location nursery, has embraced the age of technology. Their customer receipts are computerized and they even have voice mail for management. "Acceptance of it was really hard," says Minnich. "Not just for the staff, but for our customers. My grandmother is a customer; my mother is a customer. My mother was a little girl coming here. It's really a family place that has touched three or four generations. Five years ago we had a large segment of older customers. They hated change. Even when we move sections around in the nursery, we'd get yelled at. Now, since they're used to it, they find it's a better way to shop," says Minnich.

Campbell & Ferrara has their *Mission Statement* posted for customers to see. "There was discussion about this, and the reason we posted it was so we'd be held to it," says Minnich. "And we do get calls from people saying; 'well, I saw your *Mission Statement* and it said this and you didn't do this,' " he says. "It's good. We want people to call us on the carpet. The alternative is they can walk out the door and never come back. When we solve the problem, they're still our customer."

CELESTIAL SEASONINGS
MISSION STATEMENT

Our mission is to grow and dominate the U.S. specialty tea market by exceeding consumer expectations with:

The best tasting, 100% natural hot and iced teas, packaged with Celestial art and philosophy, creating the most valued tea experience.

Through leadership, innovation, focus, and teamwork we are dedicated to continuously improving value to our consumers, customers, employees, and stakeholders with a quality-first organization.

CELESTIAL SEASONINGS BELIEFS

Our Quest for Excellence

We believe that in order to make this world a better place in which to live, we must be totally dedicated to the endless quest for excellence in the important tasks which we endeavor to accomplish.

Our Products

We believe in marketing and selling healthful and naturally oriented products that nurture people's bodies and uplift their souls. Our products must be superior in quality, of good value, beautifully artistic, and philosophically inspiring.

Our Consumers and Customers

We believe that our past, current and future successes come from a total dedication to excellent service to those who buy our products. Satisfying our customer and consumer needs in a superior way is the only reason we are in business, and we shall proceed with an obsession to give wholeheartedly to those who buy our products. Our customers and consumers are king, and we are here to serve them.

Our Growth

We believe in aggressive, steady, predictable and well planned growth in sales and earnings. We are intent on building a large company that will flourish into the next century and thereafter.

Dignity of the Individual

We believe in the dignity of the individual, and we are totally committed to the fair, honest, kind, and professional treatment of all individuals and organizations with whom we work.

Our Employees

We believe that our employees develop a commitment to excellence when they are directly involved in the management of their areas of responsibility. This team effort maximizes quality results, minimizes costs, and allows our employees the opportunity to have authorship and personal satisfaction in their accomplishments, as well as sharing in the financial rewards of their individual and team efforts.

We believe in hiring above average people who have a "hands on" approach to work and quest for excellent results. In exchange, we are committed to the development of our good people by identifying, cultivating, training, rewarding, retaining and promoting those individuals who are committed to moving our organization forward.

Our Environment

We believe in fostering a working environment which promotes creativity and encourages possibility thinking throughout the organization. We plan our work to be satisfying, productive, and challenging. As such, we support an atmosphere which encourages intelligent risk taking without the fear of failure.

Our Dream

Our role at Celestial Seasonings is to play an active part in making this world a better place by unselfishly serving the public. We believe we can have a significant impact on making people's lives happier and healthier through their use of our products. By dedicating our total resources to this dream, everyone profits: our customers, consumers, employees, and shareholders. Our actions are building blocks in making this world a better place now and for future generations.

Eighty percent of the company's resources is aimed at making the mission statement happen.

Although their mission statement isn't very long, tea manufacturer Celestial Seasonings believes it contains all the important ingredients for success. "There is no one part of the *Mission Statement* that's more important than the other," says Kathryn Besemer, vice president for people. "The whole thing is very important because it gives very clear direction on what we are and are not going to do."

. . . **grow and dominate the U.S. specialty tea market** . . . "It's in there to focus us. We felt that's what we needed to focus on for the next two or three years," Besemer says. "And it wasn't at the expense of saying we won't work in international markets or other areas, it just means that a mission statement, as we believe it to mean, focuses about eighty percent of the resources you have within a company—the human resources and the financial resources. Eighty percent of your dollars should be going toward making that mission statement happen," says Besemer. "It doesn't mean that you're not looking at things outside your mission statement—other opportunities, new product lines, and new areas to be distributed—but that the bulk of your resources are focused behind that idea."

. . . **creating the most valued tea experience.** "We struggled with those words quite a bit," says Besemer. "But the concept behind the valued tea experience was that people who drink our tea don't just have a cup of tea, gulp it down, and they're out the door. The thing we hear from our consumers time and time again is that they like the artwork on the box. That's also part of the tea experience. The feeling or emotion the artwork elicits from you. One of the things Chief Executive Officer Mo Siegel talks about is wanting to create 'a feeling in the soul.' What feeling does that artwork elicit? What do the quotes make you think about? Do they make you smile? Does it make you contemplative? You have a box in your hand, you open it, you unwrap the inner liner, and there's an aroma, a smell. It's a sensual experience, it smells wonderful. It puts you in a tea state. It puts you in this mindset that I'm doing something nice for myself. Then you take the tea bag out and there's the tea; the color that the tea brews in the water, how it looks and smells, and then ultimately how it tastes and how that taste makes you feel. That's what we were trying to get at as to the tea experience. Everybody in the company has a part in doing that, from the art department to the herb buyers to the people in product development. Everybody has a role in creating the tea experience. The value, then, is bringing it to the consumer at what they think is a reasonable price for that experience."

Through leadership, innovation, focus, and teamwork . . . "We included this because six employees got together when we put the mission statement in the newsletter and offered the words *leadership, innovation, focus, teamwork*: LIFT. They thought these words so crucial that they made a banner with these words on it, passed it around for employee endorsement, and sent it to the final wordsmithing session with every employees' signature on it," says Besemer. "The leadership team sensed that it was important to integrate those words because it showed a commitment and it showed a desire to link it all together."

Celestial Seasonings is the brainchild of founder and now-returned Chief Executive Officer Mo Siegel. After a brief hiatus when he left the company, Kraft bought and sold them, and now Mo is back at the helm. "The board of directors wanted Mo to lead the company in a new era of growth," says Besemer. "Our *Beliefs* statement was in place before he left in the early eighties. Rarely should your beliefs change," she added. "The *Beliefs* statement really says who we are and how we do things. It governs our actions day in and out. If we have a question on how to proceed, we always refer to the *Beliefs* statement."

Celestial Seasonings' *Mission Statement* is different from most others in that it was designed to be used for a short term. "What's important about this mission statement is that it was intended to be in the two- to three-year range," says Besemer. "Once you have your beliefs statement, the next step is the mission. Where are we going, what are we trying to accomplish? The mission statement gives you direction and clarity."

"It [writing the corporate mission statement] was an iterative process over three months, beginning in late January 1992. Mo and I did a skeletal framework and sent it out to the leadership team. They had a couple of weeks to look at it, show it to their departments, and then they sent it back to me. Mo and I sat down and mushed it all together. Then, in the middle of March, we had a three-day strategic planning off site. The first thing we did was talk about the *Mission Statement*. I said, 'This is how it's beginning to shape up. Does it make sense?,' " recalls Besemer.

"After that meeting we put it out in the Sleepytime newsletter and told the employees: 'If you have an opinion about this, let us know what you think.' " Celestial Seasonings had 210 employees at the time and over twenty-five percent of them responded, eager to contribute to the company's new directives. "I typed up the comments and circulated them to the leadership team again, and that's when Mo and I made a draft and took it back to the company. By April it was done," she says.

The new *Mission Statement* along with the *Beliefs* statement from 1983 set the cornerstone for doing business. Every employee has his own copy of these documents which also are framed and hung throughout the building.

Besemer takes pride in the fact that Celestial Seasonings is different from many companies that follow traditional, some say old-fashioned, corporate paths. However, these documents do even things out a bit. "The *Mission Statement* is the most corporate thing we have going," she says.

Trammell Crow Company

Our Vision

To be the premier customer-driven real estate services company
in the U.S.

Guiding Principles

CUSTOMERS

We build long-term customer relationships by listening to, understanding, and exceeding our customers' needs—timely and
hassle-free.

We add value to customers' operations and provide useful information.

PEOPLE

We recruit, train, and promote the best people and are committed to quality, integrity, openness, hard work, fair compensation, innovation, diversity, respect for others, and merit.

Each person is involved and empowered, is responsible and
accountable, and is expected to learn and grow.

WORK PROCESSES

We work together in planning, setting standards, continuously improving and delivering quality services.

We work together as teams—locally, regionally, and nationally —to best serve our customers.

PROFITABILITY

We plan for steady, profitable growth in each current business, and expect to add new services and products.

We operate to build the value of the entire company for the long term.

One single word transforms a giant developer.

"We needed values that didn't change very much and a strategy that did change," says Chief Operating Officer and Chief Financial Officer Mike Decker.

Their vision statement did indeed change. One word was added, but it changed the whole texture and strategy of the company: **To be the premier customer-driven real estate services company in the U.S.**

Why?

With the real estate recession a reality in the 1980s, Trammell Crow recognized they needed to do something else besides be the foremost real estate developer as stated in their vision. So they decided to switch gears and expand into real estate *services*. The shift in focus from real estate developer to real estate services took place from 1989 to 1991 in an effort to generate revenue due to the softening real estate market. The implementation of that strategy started in 1991 and continues today. "This is the major change captured in this statement," says Decker of the additional word "services."

Before this change, *Fortune* said in 1987 that Trammell Crow (the person and the company) was "the largest non-government developer of all, consistently putting up well over $1 billion a year of trade and shopping centers, office and industrial buildings, warehouses, hotels and housing."

As for the *Guiding Principles*, the first one deals with their **Customers.** The term **hassle-free** is one you don't find very often in mission statements, too colloquial for many companies. Decker explains: "We want to be good listeners and understand what people are trying to accomplish. There's a tendency for people to believe that a developer makes decisions, then consults people to see if they like the decision. In the service business, you have to consult people to see what they want to have done and then build it. It's a big difference. We wanted to highlight that because it's a reversal of thought processes."

Adding value is something on everyone's mind these days, for both the buyer and the seller. Trammell Crow prides themselves on the network they have set up to access **useful information** for their clients. "A monthly report goes out on every asset we manage," says Decker. "Information requirements have doubled or tripled, so reports become crucial. The report that an asset manager gets is sometimes more important than what's happening to the building. 'Useful' also means formatting the report in such a way that the report is user-friendly," he says.

Trammell Crow employs 2,400 people, and this new service-oriented approach took its toll on employees. "We probably had a reduction of thirty-five percent in our workforce," says Decker. "It was a matter of goal setting and training. We had to change the way we set goals and reward goals. We had to change the training process. We used to interview based on background and what people have done. Now we interview and ask people how they would approach their job. It's a simple change, but in a one-hour discussion, the discussion is totally different. Instead of who you are and what have you done, it's what would you do."

Trammell Crow has a formalized ongoing training process called Trammell Crow University. "Once every other week we go through some advance training in service with property leasing or finance," says Decker. "We also have a set of eleven bonus criteria that are oriented toward giving good service. There's an old saying, 'you can't manage what you can't measure.' We wanted to be clear as to what we want measured," he says.

Trammell Crow has gone from a group mentality to an individual mentality as well. "There was a tendency to look for a consensus view, adopt that view, and see what happens," says Decker. "Consequently, there was group responsibility for the decision and group responsibility for the consequences. The consequences are now measured for an individual rather than the group. There's more clarity in terms of accountability and it differentiates between a top performer and a low performer. People have realized that they can manage their own destiny," he says.

They haven't completely abandoned the notion of teamwork, however, and that is covered under **Work Processes**. Trammell Crow has a "best practices sharing group" that searches across the country for the best people in each area from air-conditioning to roofing to office leasing. These teams come together when there is a problem at the asset level or at the customer level. "We found we have the most success with the most complex of situations," says Decker. "The harder it is, the more successful we tend to be. The more average the project, the more difficult it is to distinguish yourself with the outcomes."

When working with these teams, the customer has the opportunity to award an additional bonus to the team if they're happy with the outcome. "It can be as much as a couple of hundred thousand dollars," says Decker. "We usually get the bonus."

New services and products, under the **Profitability** heading is the key to their success in the future. "A whole new product line we've added is facilities management," says Decker. "As distinct from taking a downtown office building, leasing it up, and managing it, we are doing things that are much more generally oriented around the corporate facilities issue. It's a broad product line, and in the past year we've increased our management in this area by about twelve million square feet. So it's a new product, but it's really a rearrangement of the functional skills we already had. The skill set tends to be consistent over time, but the product offerings can change quite a bit," he says.

The final thought under profitability, **build the value of the entire company for the long term** represents another change in thinking for Trammell Crow. "The classical way of thinking about real estate for a developer is that you build a building and you sell the income stream on the building to someone else," says Decker. "So typically, for the developer, the big pot of gold at the end of the rainbow was the sale of the value of the building once it was filled up, based on what we call N.O.I., or net operating income, for the building. There could be an enormous amount of value creation in building an empty building and then filling it up with high-quality tenants with long-term leases. This statement rearranges all that. What we're talking about is the value of the income stream from the company as a whole. Rather than a developer thinking N.O.I. on a building, we're thinking, in a sense, N.O.I. on the entire basket of services nationwide that we provide," he says.

Dayton Hudson Corporation

OUR MISSION

We are in business to please our customers . . . to provide greater value than our competitors.

➤ By giving customers what they seek in terms of quality merchandise that is both fashion-right and competitively priced.
➤ By having the most wanted merchandise in stock and in depth in our stores.
➤ By giving customers a total shopping experience that meets or exceeds their expectations for service, convenience, environment, and ethical standards.

Everything we do—throughout our organization—should support and advance the accomplishment of this mission.

OUR MERCHANDISING PHILOSOPHY

Our merchandising philosophy is a reflection of our overall business mission —to serve our customers better than our competitors.

We believe that what the customers look for—in deciding where to shop—can be summed up in one word: value.

Our merchandising philosophy identifies five major elements of value:

➤ Quality
➤ Competitive Price
➤ Dominance of Selection
➤ Fashion
➤ Shopping Experience

Each of our companies defines "value" as it applies to its customers, and determines what role value plays in its merchandise strategy.

Each of our companies uses the principles of Trend Merchandising to identify where its customers' emphasis on value is, and how it is changing.

Trend Merchandising helps us to determine what is becoming more important to the customer and what is becoming less important—so we can allocate our resources accordingly.

OUR OPERATING PHILOSOPHY

We set high performance standards for every store in our family of companies. Good housekeeping. Service that meets or exceeds customer expectations. Clear signage. Well-organized stores with clearly presented trends.

We believe in having a clearly stated return policy throughout the corporation. No hassles. No arguments.

Retailing is a very competitive business. We are committed to managing assets profitably and to reducing expenses that do not contribute to serving our customers.

To do this, we strive to be a leader in adopting proven systems and approaches in the areas of product development, purchasing, distribution, store operations, and management information.

We seek premier locations. Our long-range success depends as much on a sound real estate strategy as it does on a sound merchandise strategy.

We have our growth priorities in order:

➤ First, we expand existing businesses in existing markets through comparable store sales increases and full market coverage.
➤ Then we expand to new markets—new geographies within the United States and eventually consideration of selected international markets.
➤ Lastly, we expand by adding new companies, either developed internally or by acquisition.

We are an honest-dealing corporation. No deceptions. No shortcuts. No gray areas. Being honest is not only right, it is good business.

MAKING A DIFFERENCE THROUGH OUR PEOPLE

Our employees make it possible for Dayton Hudson to serve others: our customers, stockholders, and communities.

They are the people who make the difference in our performance.

That is why we insist on competitive compensation, regular performance appraisals, and systematic training and development. That is why we prefer to promote from within whenever possible.

While no employer can guarantee job security, we want our people—at all levels—to have the opportunity for stable, long-term careers. This objective is best achieved when we achieve our business and financial goals.

We comply—voluntarily and fully—with the law, and with good personnel practices. We provide equal opportunity. We are committed to managing and fostering a diverse workforce. We believe ethnic and gender diversity within our workforce, as with our customers, is a strategic advantage.

Throughout Dayton Hudson, we seek a work atmosphere that encourages employee initiative and input . . . and which fosters trust and creativity.

Spelling out our responsibilities to our employees is one thing. Living up to them is quite another. We are far from perfect, and we continually challenge ourselves to become a better employer.

Each sentence is a lesson in retailing strategy.

Dayton Hudson's current pamphlet, entitled *Management Perspectives*, revised in 1992, has their mission statement on the first page. "I think everything we do is on page one," says Henry DeNero, vice chairman and chief financial officer. **We are in business to please our customers** . . . No secrets here. "Retailing is the consummate consumer business. It's hard to imagine a retail enterprise not having its mission be one that's focused around customer satisfaction and meeting or exceeding customer expectations," says DeNero.

. . . **to provide greater value than our competitors** finishes the first sentence. "Value has a very precise meaning," says DeNero. "It means you're providing a customer with a better package of product and service at the price the customer has to pay to get it. In retailing, value means fashion, quality, assortment, ease of shopping, service, and ambiance—at a certain price. The combination of all these variables either delivers a better package than the competitor does, or it doesn't. Price is always a big part of the value equation. People at all income levels are conscious of price."

DeNero explains that the company focuses on what the value is in each of its companies and then in each of the major merchandise categories. Dayton Hudson, headquartered in Minneapolis, owns and operates Dayton's, Hudson's, Marshall Field's, Target, and Mervyn's—over 900 stores in 33 states. They consider Dayton's, Hudson's, and Marshall Field's as one operating division (upscale), Target (moderate price) as the next, and Mervyn's (upscale discount) as the third. Each division serves a defined customer group with a specific strategy and operates under a common vision and management philosophy.

"It was the first time they'd ever put together anything like this," says Ann Barkelew, vice president for corporate public relations. "Dayton Hudson, at that time, was much more decentralized, with our operating companies being much more autonomous." DeNero adds, "There's been an evolution in our corporate culture away from a holding-company approach to a more integrated and more collaborative management between the corporate office and the operating companies."

. . . **having the most wanted merchandise in stock** . . . translates to Trend Merchandising, a phrase that is discussed in the pamphlet under the section titled *Our Merchandising Philosophy*. This simply means that they want to stay on top of the fashion trends so they know when something is hot and when it's not, so they can allocate their resources accordingly. "For example," says Barkelew, "if we know that bodysuits are a trend, we'll have them in greater quantity a year ahead of our competitors."

. . . **giving customers a total shopping experience** . . . is to Dayton Hudson what the "valued tea experience" is to Celestial Seasonings. Barkelew explains: "Was it convenient to park, were the service personnel friendly, was the store clean, was the merchandise easy to find, was the store easy to get around in, did we have what you came to shop for, did our people help you think of other things while you were there, was the price clearly marked, was the signage clear, did we provide the kinds of extra services you might need?"

Dayton Hudson seems to have a particular focus on the extra-services part of the total shopping experience. For example, in their department stores, customers who shop on their lunch hour might need to call their offices, so they have phones in the dressing rooms and fax machines on each floor. They provide special assistance to disabled customers. They have coat checks in the stores in colder areas of the country. The total shopping experience also includes how easy it is for a customer to return a product. "Hassling a customer is grounds for dismissal in any of our companies," says Barkelew. "We still believe the customer is always right."

Their customer's pleasure extends beyond the store walls as well. Dayton Hudson is concerned with every kind of contact that they have with the customer, from including perfume samples with the bill, or not, if that is your preference, to monitoring their advertising so as to not portray images that could offend or harm anyone.

. . . **ethical standards** also includes promoting a family atmosphere in all their stores. "When Prince came out with his album where he was naked on the cover, we didn't carry it," says Barkelew. "We don't sell any offensive material. It took about two seconds to make the Prince decision," she says.

Dayton Hudson is on the cutting edge of retail technology as well, and *Management Perspectives* addresses this point: . . . **we strive to be a leader in adopting proven systems and approaches in the areas of product development, purchasing, distribution, store operations, and management information.** For example, inventory control is done with a radio frequency scanning gun that "shoots" the bar code. The "team member" keys in how many units are on the shelf and the computer computes how many should be on the shelf for a full display and logs in how many are needed. This information is also sent to manufacturers through Electronic Data Interchange (EDI). "The manufacturer gets to know what's being sold at the retail level sooner and can adjust their production accordingly," explains DeNero.

Another new technology used by Dayton Hudson is Advanced Shipping Notice, which eliminates the time-consuming task of checking the merchandise in each box. The computer sends it on its way with automated sorting and bar coding. "When you tie all these technologies together, you get radical improvements in speed and cost and they require less inventory to provide the same level of business," DeNero says.

"Everything in *Management Perspectives* is mutually consistent and mutually supportive, flowing from the overriding mission statement of providing superior value to customers. There is a system of logic here, not just a set of unconnected desires," says DeNero.

Delta Air Lines

Worldwide Airline of Choice

Worldwide . . . We provide our customers access to the world, and we will be an innovative, aggressive, ethical and successful competitor committed to profitability and superior customer service. Looking ahead, we will consider opportunities to expand through new routes and alliances.

Airline . . . We will stay in the business we know best and where we are leaders—air transportation and related services. We believe air transportation will grow worldwide, and we will focus our time, attention and investment in building on our leadership position.

Of Choice . . . We will be the airline of choice for customers, investors and Delta people. For experienced business and leisure travelers, we will provide value and a superior travel experience from the time a reservation is made to when baggage is claimed. For air shippers, we will provide service and value. For our stockholders, we will earn a consistent, superior financial return. For Delta people, we will offer challenging, rewarding, results-oriented work in an environment that respects and values their contributions.

OUR CHALLENGE

Our challenge is to realize our vision and return to profitability. Our business has changed dramatically and forever. We have grown from a regional carrier to a worldwide airline, and we must have a broad view of Delta and ourselves as we operate in diverse markets with new customers. Throughout the world, we face innovative competitors and alliances. There is unrelenting pressure to control costs while providing excellent, high value service. Our established ways of doing business which served us well in the past will not sustain us in the future.

Our response to this challenge is to build on the strengths of our past and to create a strong, profitable future for our company as the worldwide airline of choice.

OUR STRENGTHS

Our people are Delta's competitive edge. This is our airline. Our efforts will lead Delta into the future, and each of us has a critical job to do. We work as a team, and we respect each other.

Our customer service is the cornerstone of the company. We value our customers and their needs, and we focus our energies on providing service that they value.

Our route system is strong. Delta's U.S. network is geographically balanced. We are the leading transatlantic carrier, and our Pacific routes hold significant potential.

Our operations and our fleet are outstanding. We are safe, dependable and efficient.

Our actions are ethical and honest. Our reputation is priceless, and we will not compromise our integrity.

HOW WE WILL MOVE FORWARD

We will focus with a sense of urgency and commitment on achieving superior, sustained financial results.

We will understand and be quickly responsive to our competitive, worldwide business environment, and we will be innovative competitors as we meet changing customer demands, seize market opportunities, broaden our distribution channels and influence positive regulatory change.

We will improve the quality and consistency of our service in a cost-effective way by understanding what customers value and will pay for, and then by providing it better than any other airline. We will offer a superior product at a competitive cost by becoming more cost efficient and productive.

We will have a worldwide view of our work, our company and its operations. We will continue to build our individual skills, and we will bring others with specific skills into the company when they can help us reach our vision.

We will expand the responsibility, authority and accountability of Delta people, empowering them to act quickly and decisively within their jobs. We will support this expanded authority by focusing on performance in our evaluation and compensation programs.

We will recognize and capitalize on the increasing importance of technology in every aspect of our business.

MEASUREMENT

We will set goals and measure our improvement toward them in three major areas:

Customer service. We will be Number One in customer service by becoming a leader among major airlines as measured by the Department of Transportation statistics for customer complaints, baggage handling and on-time performance. The result of providing high-value service to our customers will be improved revenues.

Market position. We will build and sustain a positive gap between our share of Revenue Passenger Miles to our share of Available Seat Miles in order to validate, market-by-market, our progress toward becoming the worldwide airline of choice.

Profitability. We will become the consistent industry leader in operating profit and net profit with a goal of ten percent operating profit and five percent net profit.

OUR REWARDS

Our vision builds on Delta's heritage, but it requires a renewed commitment from each of us to excellence and to significant, positive change. The rewards will be worth the effort. Our vision leads to sustained profitability, and that is our only security for the future, both as individuals and as a company. With profitability also comes opportunity for growth and advancement and the pride that comes from being part of an exceptional business organization. We will have the satisfaction of seeing customers come to us for service, of investors joining us to share in our vision and its rewards and of earning respect around the world. Our future requires that we become the airline of choice, and our Delta heritage demands it.

THE VISION FOR DELTA AIR LINES

Did you see a live presentation or a video presentation?

_____Live   _____Video

How well do you understand the Vision for Delta from the presentation and materials provided?

Degree of understanding

Low		Moderate		High	
1	2	3	4	5	6

Will the Vision for Delta as you understand it help you to do your job more effectively?

Effectiveness

Low		Moderate		High	
1	2	3	4	5	6

Was attending this session worthwhile for you?

Degree of worth

Low		Moderate		High	
1	2	3	4	5	6

What questions do you have about Delta and the Vision for the future?

_____
_____
_____
_____
_____
_____
_____
_____

Name _____
Station _____ Dept. _____

PLEASE DO NOT PUT THIS RESPONSE CARD IN
AN ENVELOPE UNLESS YOU WORK IN A SATO OFFICE
OR A LOCATION THAT DOES NOT HAVE ACCESS TO
COMPANY MAIL.

Short but full of intent.

Worldwide **Airline of Choice.** That is Delta's vision statement. **Worldwide . . . We provide our customers access to the world . . .** "We want Delta to be one of the major global carriers in the world. We should not be relegated to some niche," said Chairman, President, and CEO Ron Allen. "Does that mean that we're going to have our Delta pilots flying to every city in the world? No, it doesn't mean that. We'll be able to serve passengers' needs throughout the world by our own routes as well as alliances that are formed by Delta with other carriers." Creating alliances means that U.S. carriers court European and Asian carriers, and vice versa, to work together. One result of these alliances is code sharing. Code sharing means airlines buy blocks of seats on cooperating airlines and can sell tickets to every destination worldwide without having to buy planes to service all the routes. "It's like carpooling," says Tom Slocum, vice president of corporate communications, and it's essential to accomplish their "worldwide" part of the *Vision.* "What we're doing at Delta is laying out a strategic plan for us to decide whom we want to do business with and whom it makes the most sense to team up with," says Allen.

The second part of their *Vision* says they want to be an airline only. **We will stay in the business we know best . . .** "We thought it very important that we clarify for the traveling public and all the members of Delta that we're going to stay in the airline business," Allen told employees. "Our focus is going to be on running the best airline we know how."

The last section uses the words **Of Choice.** "We want to be the airline that the traveling public chooses whenever they have a choice," Allen said. "We want them to choose us because of the quality of our company, the way we maintain airplanes, the way we fly the airplanes, and the way we serve our customers."

Along with the *Vision*—the first three sections—the pamphlet goes on to talk about their challenge, their strengths, how they will move forward, how they will measure themselves and their rewards. Unlike many company mission statements that discuss keeping their leadership position, Delta talks plainly and simply about making a profit, something they haven't done in many years. **Our challenge is to realize our vision and return to profitability.** For profitability, they have set a goal of **ten percent operating profit and five percent net profit.**

To their credit, Delta has set goals that will be measured by outside, unbiased parties—as do all other airlines—giving the company no room to make excuses or play with the numbers. **Customer service. We will be Number One in customer service . . . as measured by Department of Transportation statistics for customer complaints, baggage handling and on-time performance.** "Delta has been traditionally last in on-time performance," says Slocum. We want to be in the upper middle." In the first two months of 1994, they moved from tenth to fourth place. Delta also runs the race for first place with Southwest Airlines in being the airline with the least complaints. As far as baggage handling, they're in the middle of the pack.

In their quest for market position, Delta wants to . . . **sustain a positive gap between our share of Revenue Passenger Miles to our share of Available Seat Miles . . .** In other words, no empty seats.

"We want to maintain the traditions of Delta," Allen told employees. "The last three years have been the most challenging in the airline industry and for Delta. . . . If we're satisfied with the status quo, we simply won't be here as an airline. . . . We want to be the Worldwide Airline of Choice."

Delta wants to be the choice for travelers, airline employees, and investors, but they have a long way to go. Substantial losses in 1991 and 1992 forced them to lay off pilots for the first time in 35 years, reduce wages, and cancel aircraft orders. In April 1994 Delta announced it was going to lay off 12,000 to 15,000 people and brought forth a plan to cut operating costs by $2 billion by the middle of 1997.

"The whole industry is struggling to exist in a low fare, nonregulated environment," says Slocum. "The whole process started one year ago at senior management meetings. It started at the management level, then we had groups of employees professionally facilitated in focus groups. Outside consultants helped us think of our strategic options. They suggested we have a vision statement." The development of the vision statement took eight months.

"The name of the game around here today is change," said Chairman Ron Allen during a nine-city "vision tour" in late 1993, naming it the "Delta Vision Roadshow." He met with 12,000 employees face-to-face in meetings that took place in airport hangers set up with a stage. Videotapes were made of the sessions and sent to the Delta sites that Allen couldn't visit personally.

Their vision pamphlet has been given to all employees. This pamphlet has a tear-on-the-dotted-line panel that asks question of employees such as Did you see a live presentation or a video presentation? How well do you understand the *Vision* for Delta? Will the *Vision* . . . help you to do your job more effectively? and, perhaps most important of all, Was attending the session worthwhile for you? There is also a section where employees can ask questions. The nonanonymous card was to be mailed in, and the tabulated results showed a "high" degree (78 percent) of understanding, effectiveness, and worth for the live show. Results were lower for the video show (48 percent rated it in the "high" level).

But first they have to get through the storm clouds and into the blue skies. "These tough times we're going through right now will actually make us a much better airline, and that's what we want to be," Allen told employees. "We want to be the best airline."

Tom Slocum recalls that one business traveler on a Delta flight told him recently, "My office is seat 3B, and I want my office to run right."

Gannett

Game Plan as of April 1, 1989

- To make acquisitions in news, information, and communications and closely related fields, like entertainment or advertising, that make economic sense.
- To get a return on them in three or more years with the emphasis on three, but recognizing those with high growth potential may cost more initially.
- To expand and create products in related areas, such as *USA Today* spin-off summaries via New Media. Other examples are the discussions about taking our twice-weekly North Hills newspapers daily as a first or final edition or separate edition of the *Valley News Dispatch*. Also, we are studying the Fairpress, in Fairfield, to determine the feasibility of a Sunday edition. It is now published on Wednesdays.
- To emphasize as a first priority increased profitability and increased return on equity and investment.
- To enhance the quality of all our products, to help achieve those levels of profitability and return and to protect the editorial integrity of our products.

John J. Curley

Game Plan as of October 2, 1991

- To make acquisitions in news, information, and communications and closely related fields that make economic sense.
- To get a return on them in three or more years with the emphasis on three, but recognizing those with high growth potential may cost more initially.

- To expand and create products in related areas under the New Media umbrella.
- To emphasize as a first priority increased profitability and increased return on equity and investment.
- To enhance the quality of all our products, to help achieve those levels of profitability and return and to protect the editorial integrity of our products. Better products will mean better profits.
- To dispose of assets that have limited or no potential and those that have peaked and are trending down.

Game Plan as of August 24, 1992

- To create, improve, and expand products through innovation and continue to make acquisitions in news, information, and communications and related fields that make strategic and economic sense.
- To get a positive return on new and acquired products and properties in a reasonable period of time, while recognizing those with high growth potential may take more time.
- To emphasize as priorities:
  - ➢ Increased profitability and increased return on equity and investment over the long term.
  - ➢ Enhance quality and the editorial integrity of our products, recognizing that quality products ultimately lead to higher profits.
  - ➢ Respect for and fairness in dealing with employees.
  - ➢ A diverse environment where opportunity is based on merit.
  - ➢ Commitment and service to communities where we do business.
  - ➢ Customer satisfaction.
  - ➢ Disposing of assets that have limited or no potential.

Game Plan as of August 23, 1993

BUSINESS DEFINITION

Gannett is a $3.5 billion news, information, and communications company.

We operate with the belief that improving products and sound management will lead to higher profits for our shareholders.

The underlying theme in our ads is: "A world of different voices where freedom speaks."

Our assets include:

- *USA Today*
- Daily and weekly community newspapers and specialty publications
- Television and radio stations in Top 25 and growth markets
- Out-of-home and in-home media products.

STRATEGIC VISION

- Create and expand quality products through innovation
- Make acquisitions in news, information, and communications and related fields that make strategic and economic sense.

OPERATING PRINCIPLES

- Provide effective leadership and efficient management
- Achieve a positive return on new and acquired products and properties in a reasonable period of time, while recognizing those with high growth potential may take more time
- Increase profitability and increase return on equity and investment over the long term

- Enhance the quality and editorial integrity of our products, recognizing that quality products ultimately lead to higher profits
- Guarantee respect for and fairness in dealing with employees
- Offer a diverse environment where opportunity is based on merit
- Show commitment and service to communities where we do business
- Deliver customer satisfaction
- Dispose of assets that have limited or no potential
- In all activities we show respect for the First Amendment and our responsibility to it.

Like its newspapers, the *Game Plan* changes to fit with the times.

"We call it our *Game Plan* and we didn't have one written before 1989," says Chairman John Curly. "But when Al Neuharth retired, one of our directors, Julian Goodman, the chairman of NBC, suggested that we ought to write down what the game plan was. So I wrote it—I banged it out and took the collective wisdom and circulated it to the board and management committee. After the first one I said I would come back every year for possible changes. Give you a shot of what you'd like to see, but remember the size of this thing. I really want to make it workable," says Curly, whose company publishes 83 daily newspapers, including *USA Today* and more than 50 nondaily publications. Gannett owns and operates ten television stations, six FM and five AM radio stations, and Gannett Outdoor Group, the largest billboard/outdoor poster company.

Gannett's *Game Plan* shows a steady progression and growth of ideas from 1989 to now. Along the way, certain points were highlighted while others were changed to reflect new economic realities.

From the 1989 and 1991 *Game Plans*: **To get a return** [on acquisitions] **in three or more years with the emphasis on three, but recognizing those with high growth potential may cost more initially.** This was changed in 1992 to: **To get a positive return on new and acquired products and properties in a reasonable period of time, while recognizing those with high growth potential may take more time.**

"We used three years because that was the time focus in those days on doing deals. A deal made sense if we could break even in three years. What happened is that the frenzy of deal making was still escalating. Simultaneously, we began to see national advertising collapse. We realized that the better deals would take more than three years to get back to even, but we wanted to keep it as the benchmark anyway. Later on we would be willing to give more time if it was a really good opportunity. The 1991 *Game Plan* was less specific and more of a recognition of elements outside our control," Curly says.

Curly says the change in wording wasn't aimed specifically at justifying the long time it took *USA Today* to make money. Started in 1982, *USA Today* is now the largest-circulation newspaper in the United States, bypassing *The Wall Street Journal* in 1992. After ten years of losses exceeding $700 million, *USA Today* has turned the corner. On the other hand, *Baseball Weekly*, launched in 1991, has taken less than three years to get in the black, according to Curly.

One economic theme constant in the *Game Plan* since 1991 has to do with disposing of properties that aren't producing well. **To dispose of assets that have limited or no potential and those that have peaked and are trending down** (1991); **Disposing of assets that have limited or no potential** (1992, 1993).

"We're always looking at properties that may have run their course or are not effective. It may not have anything to do with the person running it, but the market may have gone south or something else, but they could be up for sale. We probably startled a few people by saying that we were going to clean some stuff out—and we have. It doesn't mean we sell them all, but it means that we're going to look at them," says Curly.

Another important change came in the 1992 version. **To emphasize as priorities . . . Respect for and fairness in dealing with employees.** "Quite simply, we decided that we wanted to highlight that point."

Ironically, Gannett had never mentioned the First Amendment— freedom of the press—in its *Game Plan* until the 1993 version. **In all activities we show respect for the First Amendment and our responsibility to it.** Says Curly: "I should have had that in earlier. It was an oversight on my part, given that I'm a newsperson. I wanted to make it clear that we weren't going to knuckle under to people who thought they could say 'look the other way.' We wanted people to know that we will go after stories when they're out there."

USA Today has often come under criticism for being oriented toward "soft news" without depth. This mention of the First Amendment was meant, in part, to counter some of these criticisms. "This change also came at a time of our News 2000 initiative, making our papers more readable and accessible, but I wanted people to know that we would still go after the tough stories. I wanted to make it clear to the newsrooms that they've got to do their jobs in that area," Curly notes.

In 1993 the *Game Plan* became more modular, a little bit easier to read and interpret. Ideas were classified into sections: *Business Definition, Strategic Vision,* and *Operating Principles.* It's also the first time that the company's assets, such as *USA Today,* were listed. The idea, according to Curly, was to make the *Game Plan* more readable—just like the newspapers.

And what's going to be the next change? "I look at the *Game Plan* every summer," Curly says. "We've got one suggestion for next year, but I don't know if we're going to do it. Some people think we should move customer satisfaction up, but I'm inclined to leave it where it is because I think that in the category it's in *(Operating Principles),* all of these items should get equal weight so it doesn't matter where it is."

What's the most important part? "The underlying theme is that better products and sound management will lead to higher profits. In twenty-five words or less, that's the most important part, says Curly. **We operate with the belief that improving products and sound management will lead to higher profits for our shareholders.**

Nineteen words to be exact.

GEICO

GEICO's Mission Is:

To market quality personal insurance services at a price and service advantage through direct response mechanisms, and, where appropriate, through general field representatives.

VISION STATEMENT

This is a statement of why we exist and what we want to be.

GEICO exists because we provide our customers a peace-of-mind guarantee that their assets and income are protected from financial loss, if an event which they fear shall occur.

And, we provide certain other customers the evidence that they have met their state's minimum financial responsibility and legal requirements to operate a motor vehicle.

We will be recognized as the leader in providing quality insurance products and services by all who associate with GEICO in any matter.

To obtain this distinction, we will:

- Earn and maintain the loyalty and respect of our customers and associates.
- Conduct our business affairs with uncompromising honesty and integrity.
- Be innovative and resourceful in meeting customers' needs.
- Remain open to new ideas and adaptive to change.
- Achieve and maintain the lowest possible level of cost and price.
- Promote traffic, home and boating safety.
- Serve our customers through properly trained associates.
- Maximize associates' opportunities for personal development and growth.

- Involve all associates as problem solvers and solution implementers.
- Recognize achievements and celebrate them.
- Be recognized as a responsible corporate citizen.

GEICO'S FIVE OPERATING PRINCIPLES

- be fanatics for good service
- maintain a disciplined balance sheet
- be the low-cost operator
- achieve an underwriting gain
- invest for total return.

They stick to it, even if it means selling off some units.

"On May 5, 1976, Jack Byrne became chairman and president during a time of financial crisis," says Dave Anderson, director of planning for GEICO (Government Employee Insurance Company). "The first thing he did was institute a planning process, and the mission statement came out of that process."

GEICO's original mission statement said that **GEICO's mission is to market, through direct response mechanisms, high quality insurance at competitive prices to preferred risk customers.** However, the mission statement didn't address GEICO's other businesses: GEICO General Insurance Company, GEICO Indemnity, and GEICO Casualty. These companies provide insurance for preferred-risk private passenger automobiles and for government employees and military personnel in addition to homeowners and other lines of insurance for qualified applicants. "The new statement now covers all our companies," says Anderson. The mission is still very specific though.

To market quality personal insurance . . . : GEICO doesn't insure groups at all. It's strictly an individual policy company.

. . . **direct response mechanisms** . . . : "GEICO doesn't operate through a sales force," says Anderson. "We advertise through newspaper and radio, thereby eliminating the middleman. We are the largest direct writer company in the U.S. It saves money for us and the customer. If we don't have to pay an agent's commission, we can sell the insurance at a lower price," he says.

. . . **general field representatives** . . . : "Back around 1961 the Defense Department came to GEICO and asked if we would set up a subsidiary company to offer auto insurance to the military," says Anderson. "That's when we set up GEICO Indemnity. We quickly found out that military personnel preferred to deal with agents instead of doing business over the phone or in the mail like our preferred risk customers. The military personnel dealt in cash for the most part, so we contract with agents, known as general field representatives or independent agents. These agents represent GEICO for auto insurance," he says. "Then in the mid-eighties we decided to also let those people offer the GEICO product to those who qualified for it. However, the large majority of GEICO preferred risk insurance is still sold through direct response advertising. Because this new mission statement covers all four companies, we felt it important to include the phrase 'where appropriate.'"

"Our *Mission* is tied to our *Operating Principles*, and you can't separate them. In 1977 Jack Byrne and his new management group came up with the last four points," says Anderson. The first point was added later on in 1986—**be fanatics for good service.** "At that time, we felt we needed to spend more time and focus more attention on service." Anderson goes on to say, "We always treated these principles as equals. Then, in 1987, we moved service to the highest priority." GEICO added **service advantage** to their *Mission* in 1994 to reflect this change as well.

"One out of two of GEICO's 7500 employees can recite the five operating principles. It's in all our publications and hangs on our walls throughout the building. The *Operating Principles* are the one thing everybody knows," says Anderson. "The mission statement is known by all management associates."

The mission statement is reviewed in GEICO's "challenge sessions" which are held at the end of every year. "The president produces a planning document in the summer, and each operating department is responsible for a business plan for the following year. Over a two-week period all thirty managers review each other's plans along with the senior executives. Our corporate business plan comes out of these plans," Anderson explains.

In 1991, GEICO, which has been in the same business since 1936, purchased Southern Heritage, a property-casualty insurer based in Atlanta, and Merastar, a Chattanooga, Tennessee–based company that markets employer-sponsored insurance plans. "The board of directors felt it was worth exploring other distribution systems," says Anderson. "GEICO's main thrust is in large urban areas (they are headquartered in Washington, D.C.). We viewed this as a way of getting into the rural market, where there are many preferred risk clients also." Stated in GEICO's *Vision Statement:* **Remain open to new ideas and adaptive to change.**

However, in October 1993, GEICO Chairman Bill Snyder said he was taking early retirement and announced plans to purchase Southern Heritage and Merastar from GEICO, in partnership with former GEICO Chairman Jack Byrne. When the sale of these companies was made public, they referred back to the mission statement which called for GEICO to sell only **personal insurance . . . through direct response mechanisms . . .**

"The mission statement is not everything we do, but it's the essence of what we do," adds Anderson.

General Electric

Boundaryless . . . Speed . . . Stretch

Three words say it all.

When we asked General Electric officials for a senior manager to comment about their "three words," they closed ranks and referred us to management's "letters to shareholders," in which John F. Welch, Jr., chairman and chief executive officer, wrote about his vision of GE for the 1990s. "They say everything anybody needs to know; they are straight from the chairman's mouth," a company spokesman told us. Indeed they were.

General Electric's mission statement contains just three words: **boundaryless, speed,** and **stretch.**

As Welch puts it in his 1993 annual corporate message: "We use three operating principles to define the atmosphere and behavior at GE: **boundaryless** . . . in all our behavior; **speed** . . . in everything we do; **stretch** . . . in every target we set."*

"Boundaryless behavior is the soul of today's GE," stated Welch. "Simply put, people seem compelled to build layers and walls between themselves and others, and that human inclination tends to be magnified in large old institutions like ours. These walls cramp people, inhibit creativity, waste time, restrict vision, smother dreams, and, above all, slow things down. The challenge is to chip away at and eventually break down walls and barriers, both among ourselves and between ourselves and the outside world. The progress we've made so far has released a flood of ideas that is improving every operation in our company," he wrote.

One of the concepts operating under the boundaryless philosophy is "Work-Out," a series of "town meetings" that bring together employees in all aspects of one of GE's businesses. The goal is to get people to examine the process of their business, identify the crucial ones, discard the rest, and find a faster, simpler, better way of doing things. Then, Welch says, "the teams raise the bar of excellence by testing their

---

* From 1989 through 1992 Welch used the first two words to describe GE's principles. In 1993 he added **stretch.**

improved processes against the very best from around the company and from the best companies around the world."

The concept of **boundaryless** behavior has resulted in more cooperation among GE divisions. For example, someone from their appliances business in Hong Kong helped NBC with contacts needed to develop a satellite television service in Asia. "Boundaryless behavior combines twelve huge global businesses—each number one or number two in its markets—into a vast laboratory whose principal product is new ideas, coupled with a common commitment to spread them throughout the company," said Welch.

Speed, the second of the three key philosophies, is something not usually found in a company the size of GE. But you'll find it there today in the form of new product development, the redesigning of their order-to-remittance cycle, or redefining capacity by reducing plant and equipment investment. For example, "in the past three years, GE's faster pace has freed up nearly five million square feet of manufacturing space across the Company," said Welch. "To a business like plastics, that has meant a savings of nearly one-half billion dollars that would have been required for new capacity—like getting a new plant free."

Stretch, the final concept, means using dreams to set business targets with no plan of how to get there. "Stretch allows organizations to set the bar higher than they ever dreamed possible," according to Welch. "The openness, candor, and trust of a boundaryless, fast company allows us to hang those dreams out there, in view of everyone, so that we can all reach for them together."

Thomas Edison wouldn't recognize the company he began in 1878. For that matter, most people who studied General Electric in the 1980s wouldn't recognize the company today either. The metamorphosis that GE has undergone is due largely to Jack Welch.

Welch has had success with mission statements before. When he became CEO in 1981 his mission was to fix the "hardware" side of the company. He examined the finances, performance, and management structure of every GE business and concluded that they wanted to be in a business only if they could be number one or number two in that market. If a given business couldn't be "fixed" to meet this standard, it was sold or closed. This plan resulted in the sale of many GE businesses, including the flagship consumer appliances division. At the same time, GE invested $17 billion in acquiring businesses such as NBC, and strengthening their current strongholds by adding companies such as Borg-Warner Chemicals to the GE Plastics Division; Montgomery Ward Credit and Kidder, Peabody to GE Financial Services; the French medical equipment company CGR to GE Medical Systems; and Tungsram of Hungary to GE Lighting. This period of sale and acquisition honed their focus to thirteen (now twelve) businesses, each number one or number two in the global market and substantially reduced the management layers in those business areas.

The effect this had on GE personnel was horrendous and began the process of change on what Welch refers to as the "software" of the company—the people of GE. The workforce of the company, trimmed almost in half since 1981—Welch cut more than 100,000 jobs—has helped double revenues from $26 billion to $60 billion. His ruthlessness in cutting jobs earned him the nickname "Neutron Jack" (which he dislikes intensely), as he was likened to the bomb developed several decades ago that kills people but leaves buildings standing.

It's the "three words" that set the tone, the pace, and the direction for GE now and in the years to come. "**Boundaryless, Speed, Stretch** . . . putting this all together: boundaryless people, excited by speed and inspired by stretch dreams, have an absolutely infinite capacity to improve everything," said Welch.

General Mills
The Company of Champions

Statement of Corporate Values

- CONSUMERS—*Consumers choose General Mills because we offer competitively superior products and services.*
- EMPLOYEES—*Employees choose General Mills because we reward innovation and superior performance and release their power to lead.*
- INVESTORS—*Investors choose General Mills because we consistently deliver financial results in the top 10 percent of all major companies.*

Our heritage and commitment to outstanding accomplishment has made General Mills "The Company of Champions." Each of us at General Mills must strive to exemplify the values that distinguish us as a unique and special company.

PRODUCTS AND SERVICES

We will provide competitively superior products and services to our customers and consumers. This superiority will be measured by rigorous, comparative testing versus the best competitive offerings and by growth in market shares.

Providing championship products and services is a never-ending job requiring continuous improvement ahead of competition.

PEOPLE AND ORGANIZATION

General Mills' people will be the best in our industries—people who are winners, ever striving to exceed their past accomplishments. Exceptional performance is the result of these people working together in small and fluid teams on those issues where success will clearly widen our competitive advantage.

We value diversity and will create workplaces where people with diverse skills, perspectives, and backgrounds can exercise leadership and help those around them release their full power and potential.

We will minimize organizational levels and have broad spans of responsibility. We will drive out bureaucracy and parochialism. We will trust each other and have the self-confidence to challenge and accept challenge.

INNOVATION

Innovation is the principal driver of growth. Innovation requires a bias for action. To be first among our competitors, we must constantly challenge the status quo and be willing to experiment. The anticipation and creation of change, both in established businesses and in new products and services, is essential for competitive advantage.

We recognize that change—and risk—are inherent to innovation. Our motivation system will strongly reward successful risk-taking, while not penalizing an innovative idea that did not work.

SPEED

We will be the fastest moving and most productive competitor. We will set specific goals to improve our speed and productivity each year compared to our own past performance and to the competition.

COMMITMENT

Our commitment to our shareholders is to deliver financial results that place us in the top 10 percent of all major companies. This can only be accomplished with the personal commitment of each of us.

The persistency to bounce back from disappointments, the intensity to pursue the exceptionally difficult, and the reliability to deliver promised results are all part of our commitment to our shareholders, to each other, and to our pride in "The Company of Champions." This commitment is demonstrated by substantial and increasing levels of employee stock ownership.

CITIZENSHIP

We will have significant positive impact on our communities. We will focus on specific projects where our efforts will make a difference in direct philanthropy, in our corporate investment in nonprofit ventures, and through our own personal involvement in civic and community affairs.

Maker of the "Breakfast of Champions," wants to be the "Company of Champions."

H.B. Atwater, Jr., now chairman of the board and chief executive officer, wrote the General Mills *Statement of Corporate Values* in 1978 when he was president. After an hour's conversation with top executives, they banged out a first draft. They got some feedback and finalized it. Atwater believes the company's *Statement of Corporate Values* is a living document that evolves over the years. However, the basic thrust remains the same. He is quick to say that these values were not invented by the group, they were just codifying what they felt the company represented.

The first section—*Products and Services*—is the most important section of the document. Atwater says when they have business meetings, the main questions are How does the product stack up against the competitor's? and How does the service stack up? Making sure they have **competitively superior products** is tested constantly through blind testing against other companies' products. Atwater says they expect to be better than their competitors' products, and if they aren't, all the alarm bells go off in research and marketing. Competitive superiority against the niche is absolutely fundamental. It's great for the consumer, he notes, because when their product is superior in a niche, the competitor tries to make their product better.

People and Organization, the next section, addresses the logistics of how the company operates. Atwater says they've always been entrepreneurial oriented because of the nature of their product line, but also because that's the way they want the company to operate. Nobody likes bureaucracy at General Mills, least of all Atwater, and he says big companies tend to get hardening of the arteries. This section of the statement also talks about driving out **bureaucracy and parochialism.** The management at General Mills believes that these two concepts, along with functionalism, the idea that one does only what one's main function or job description is instead of whatever it takes to get the job done, are the greatest organizational dangers. Atwater says "empowerment" is today's word and because of the way General Mills is organized, it's difficult for an executive committee to tell a product manager what to do because they simply have too many products. He says before the word empowerment was conceived, General Mills was running that way and has continued to do so.

The phrases in this section, **small and fluid teams . . . We value diversity and will create workplaces where people with diverse skills, perspectives, and backgrounds can exercise leadership and help those around them release their full power and potential,** all point to a very different way of doing business. Atwater says they like arguing with each other, but he believes that necessity is the mother of invention and that General Mills employees work hard to make sure the necessity is on the ideas and not on people's personalities.

The next three sections—*Innovation, Speed,* and *Commitment*—are the three drivers of the statement. Atwater points out that these three words are on the front cover of the 1993 annual report and are the focus of the letter from the executive team on the inside cover. He also says that the only major change in the values document was separating speed and innovation, which were formerly under one heading.

He notes that innovation is about risk-taking and says that if you're pushing the edge of the envelope and not stubbing your toe, then you're not pushing hard enough. If everything you've got works, then you should be worried. An example of corporate innovation is their joint venture with Nestlé, S.A., in establishing Cereal Partners Worldwide, or CPW, which is the second-largest cereal company outside North America. Their main competition is Kellogg.

The *Speed* is self-evident, according to Atwater. Do it today, not tomorrow.

The *Commitment* section deals primarily with the company's shareholders, but is directed to the employees because this is where people can run into obstacles. That's why they included phrases like **the persistency to bounce back from disappointments.**

General Mills gives stock options to everyone who has been working there for three years. Atwater believes commitment is stronger when you have ownership. The section starts out with the company's commitment to be in the top ten percent. Atwater says almost every company he knows of talks about performance in the top quarter, so he wanted to do better.

The final section concerns *Citizenship*. Eighty-five percent of General Mills employees who have been with the company more than a couple of years volunteer in a meaningful way. He says they promote community service for good business reasons—people who have the breadth to be interested in volunteering make better business executives. On the flip side, he says better people want to work for companies that are socially responsible.

General Mills's thinking was typical among the great companies in the 1970s. Diversification was the key, and General Mills got into everything from Eddie Bauer to Parker Brothers. In the 1980s, after their *Statement of Corporate Values* was written, they decided to focus on the two major enterprises that offered the greatest potential for growth and profitability: consumer foods and restaurants. Today General Mills owns the Red Lobster and Olive Garden restaurant chains and manufactures literally thousands of consumer food products, including Wheaties, Cheerios, and the Betty Crocker line.

Atwater says this *Statement of Corporate Values* is not something they stick in a file. They use it frequently in recruiting. They tell recruits to read it, and if they're not comfortable with this type of thing, then they're not right for General Mills.

Georgia-Pacific
Vision

Being the Best At Everything We Do

Georgia-Pacific is a publicly owned forest products company. As employees of a public company, our ultimate responsibility is to increase the value of our shareowners' investment. We will generate the best investment returns in our industry by focusing on our core businesses of building products, and pulp, and paper; by developing our people and our assets; and by fostering an environment that encourages change and innovation and rewards performance. We will be a company of "good people doing the right things." To outperform our competitors and to generate the best investment returns, some of the right things are to:

Provide a Safe Working Environment
and Rewarding Careers for Our Employees

Provide Customers with Products and Services
that Meet or Exceed Expectations

Promote Environmental Stewardship

Improve Operations and Products Continually

Pursue Aggressively Being the Best
at Everything We Do and Always Uphold
the Highest Standards of Business Conduct

Our Strategy for Success
Corporate Commitments and Goals

Georgia-Pacific will be committed to excellence in manufacturing and marketing of our forest products and administration of our businesses, in developing our employees and in environmental stewardship. Our vision will become reality through the following corporate commitments. Execution will make the difference.

Georgia-Pacific Will Provide an Environment
for the Development of Our Employees.

Georgia-Pacific Will Generate the Best
Investment Returns in the Industry.

Georgia-Pacific Will Lead the
Industry in International Competitiveness.

Georgia-Pacific Will Assure Leadership in Its Environmental
Performance and Apply Leading Technology and Scientific
Information to Environmental Solutions.

Georgia-Pacific Will Be a Leader in Practicing Responsible
Commercial Forestry.

Georgia-Pacific Will Consistently
Meet or Exceed Its Customers' Expectations.

"Good people doing the right things."

"The *Vision* is the global picture," says Shelia Weidman, senior manager of corporate communications for Georgia-Pacific, who is responsible for disseminating these documents to employees. "The *Corporate Commitments and Goals* was developed to explain to people a bit more of what we wanted to achieve and focus on, but to provide a little more direction than the *Vision*."

Georgia-Pacific was founded in 1927. In 1993 they developed their first vision statement. The development of this statement was part of the CEO transition when Pete Correll took office. He made the rounds of employees discovering what they wanted. This information was collected and circulated to operating officers for their comments. The next step was disseminating the statement to their 50,000 employees. Now reenforcement is the issue. "It's challenging for the employees because their commitment is stronger and they're becoming more intricately involved and they are decision makers as well as participants in decisions," Weidman explains.

In the following sections, Weidman walks us through the *Vision* and the *Corporate Commitments and Goals*.

The *Vision*

Being the Best at Everything We Do. "This is the result of achieving our *Vision*," says Weidman. "If we achieve our *Vision* and achieve our *Commitments and Goals* we believe that we will undoubtedly be the best at everything we do because the other elements are all factors of being the best. So we have a commitment to be the best and that includes employing the highest moral and business ethics," she says.

. . . our ultimate responsibility is to increase the value of our shareowners' investment. "That's a very strong philosophy at Georgia-Pacific," says Weidman. "It had grown to be very serious under the tenure of our past CEO, and all of our compensation packages are tied to shareholder value. We don't get bonuses here in this company unless the shareholder is benefiting financially as well."

We will generate the best investment returns in our industry by focusing on our core businesses of building products, pulp, and paper. "I know we generate a significantly better return than the industry average," says Weidman. Their direct competitors are Weyerhaeuser and International Paper. "We have a better than average return on investment, but it's not the best yet."

As for the core businesses focus, that's still new. "When Marshall Hahn joined us in the early eighties, the company went through a lot of reorganization and restructuring to refocus itself on the core business and sell off all the other businesses we had gotten involved in," she says. "Everything we have now is derived from the forest, so we are pretty well focused. In the eighties we were in the chemical business and the oil and gas business. We determined they weren't strategic."

We will be a company of "good people doing the right things." "This also comes from the new CEO. He believes the employees here needed clearer direction. If they're not doing their job well, it's not because they're bad people, it's because they've not been informed," says Weidman.

Promote Environmental Stewardship. "In the past for our industry and our company, environmental compliance was the standard," says Weidman. "That philosophy isn't good enough any longer. We are now working very hard to go well beyond compliance to the point where we are the forest products industry leader in environmental stewardship."

Corporate Commitments and Goals

Georgia-Pacific Will Lead the Industry in International Competitiveness. "It's always the name of the game in this industry," says Weidman. "We are basically in commodity products—plywood, pulp, lumber, photocopying paper. There aren't great quality differences from one company to the next in commodity products, so you build customer loyalty and leadership through service and cost. We have to meet and exceed customer expectations and be the low-cost producer. It's a bidding game. Cost is everything," she says.

Georgia-Pacific Will Be a Leader in Practicing Responsible Commercial Forestry. "Our Forestry for the '90's program is where you lay out all the management practices needed for compliance and you determine, on a region-by-region or state-by-state basis, what you want to do to go beyond compliance, like larger streamside zones, more selective cutting, more set-asides," says Weidman. "Our plan for the endangered red cockaded woodpeckers that we announced in 1993 with Interior Secretary Bruce Babbitt is a model of public and private initiative. We are the exclusive forestry company in this project on our own four million acres of land." She continues. "It's an example of going well beyond what's necessary. Moving beyond compliance to being proactive."

Gerber

The Mission

The people and resources of the Gerber Products Company are dedicated to assuring that the company is the world leader in, and advocate for, infant nutrition, care, and development.

THE MISSION WILL BE ACHIEVED BY:

- setting and measuring business objectives in the context of this mission;
- investing in continued product and body-of-knowledge, innovation, and research in the areas of infant nutrition, care, and development;
- providing products and services to consumers which adhere to high quality and safety standards, and at a reasonable cost;
- providing consumers and professionals with information which promotes the highest standards of infant nutrition, care, and development;
- adhering to a code of marketing practices and serving as a good citizen in all communities where the company conducts business;
- and investing in the continued development and well-being of Gerber associates.

THE ACCOMPLISHMENT OF THE MISSION IS INTENDED TO PROVIDE:

- healthy starts in the lives of all children served by Gerber;
- above average returns on the investment of Gerber's long-term shareholders;
- and rewarding employment for Gerber associates.

Think of the baby first, and you can't go wrong.

"The mission statement itself you see today is a modern re-creation of the one that Dan Gerber wrote in 1935," says Chairman, President, and Chief Executive Officer Al Piergallini. "The key element is that we do what's right for the baby. Everything always stems from that notion," says Piergallini. The mission statement states: **The people and resources of the Gerber Products Company are dedicated to assuring that the company is the world leader in, and advocate for, infant nutrition, care, and development.**

The famous Gerber baby is pictured on the mission statement, and the original charcoal drawing still exists, says Piergallini, held in a safe place. The baby has been used in advertising and on labels since the early 1930s, a few years after Dan Gerber had a baby and talked his wife into letting him strain the infant's food at his family's factory— The Fremont Canning Company. Gerber decided to sell the food commercially and sales increased during the following years. The company became the Gerber Products Company in 1941 and produced baby foods exclusively.

Tim Croasdaile, the company's vice president of corporate affairs, helped in preparation of the modern mission statement four years ago. "In order to make it a reflection of what we are, we interviewed our employees, our associates, and it was a summation of our culture. We really didn't have to do much. The mission itself flowed from what people were saying. Again, the key element is advocacy of the baby."

One major change in the mission statement's concept was in serving shareholders: . . . **above average returns on the investment of Gerber's long-term shareholders.** "In 1928, when Dan Gerber began making baby food, there was only one shareholder, Dan himself. Now we have to talk about return on investment for shareholders," Piergallini says.

The mission statement also discusses another important aspect of Gerber's philosophy—studying and sharing research on infant nutrition: . . . **investing in continued product and body-of-knowledge,**

innovation, and research in the areas of infant nutrition, care, and development. "This idea is from the early days of the company. When they first made baby food they took it to doctors for comments and suggestions. It was their way of investing in the body-of-knowledge, innovation, and research." In addition, Dan Gerber also began distributing information about infant nutrition and care in the early 1930s. Today Gerber maintains the world's largest private research facility dedicated to infant nutrition.

"Later on we added the part about the 'care' business in this section and in the mission statement itself because it didn't exist in 1928." Piergallini is referring to the company's Baby Care line of nipples, dishes, and nursing supplies which was added in 1950. The apparel group was added in 1960.

. . . providing products and services to consumers which adhere to high quality and safety standards and at a reasonable cost. "We would always look at creating products that have the highest safety standards. We have had a program in place for almost twenty years about chemicals on crops. Our standard is 'no detectable' pesticides on our baby food products. Nobody can make that claim. We did it without any regulation long before the federal government focused on it," says Piergallini.

Fiscal 1993 was not a great one for Gerber. Earnings per share declined 9.4 percent from the year before, the U.S. baby food business experienced a volume decline of five percent, and total return to investors was a negative 8.3 percent. On the other hand, cash flow from operations was almost 20 percent of revenues (the goal is a minimum of 15 percent), Gerber Childrenswear rebounded despite two facility fires to meet expectations, and the international sector, especially in Poland and Latin America, scored excellent gains.

"Although we have short-term aberrations, long-term commitment to the mission statement allows us to bring the company back and continue to move forward," says Piergallini. "The mission statement is important, because if you lose fact of the standard then you lose focus on the business. This allows us to see what the company is all about." Not withstanding recent problems, including a short-term downturn in the number of baby births and sale of its Buster Brown shoe division, which was being buffeted by low-price competitors, Gerber maintains a 70-plus share of the domestic baby food market. That type of presence is difficult to duplicate in any industry.

Amid the statistics, data, and numbers in the 1993 annual report, Piergallini summed up Gerber's future this way: "In the final analysis, our success depends upon our ability to provide the best possible products for babies. . . . By remaining faithful to this commitment, we will build the Gerber franchise globally and achieve our financial goals."

Gillette

Mission

Our mission is to achieve or enhance clear leadership, worldwide, in the existing or new core consumer product categories in which we choose to compete.

CURRENT CORE CATEGORIES ARE:

- Male grooming products including blades and razors, electric shavers, shaving preparations, and deodorants and antiperspirants.
- Selected female grooming products including wet shaving, hair removal and hair care appliances, deodorants and antiperspirants, and party-plan skin care and cosmetic products.
- Writing instruments and correction products.
- Certain areas of the oral care market including toothbrushes, interdental devices, and oral care appliances.
- Selected areas of the high-quality small household appliance business, including coffeemakers and food preparation products.

To achieve this mission, we will also compete in supporting product areas that enhance the company's ability to achieve or hold the leadership position in core categories.

VALUES

In pursuing our mission, we will live by the following values:

PEOPLE. We will attract, motivate, and retain high-performing people in all areas of our business. We are committed to competitive, performance-based compensation, benefits, training, and personal growth based on equal career opportunity and merit. We expect integrity, civility, openness, support for others, and commitment to the highest standards of achievement. We value innovation, employee involvement, change, organizational flexibility, and personal mobility. We recognize and value the benefits in the diversity of people, ideas, and cultures.

CUSTOMER FOCUS.   We will invest in and master the key technologies vital to category success. We will offer consumers products of the highest levels of performance for value. We will provide quality service to our customers, both internal and external, by treating them as partners, by listening, understanding their needs, responding fairly, and living up to our commitments. We will be a valued customer to our suppliers, treating them fairly and with respect. We will provide these quality values consistent with improving our productivity.

GOOD CITIZENSHIP.   We will comply with applicable laws and regulations at all government levels wherever we do business. We will contribute to the communities in which we operate and address social issues responsibly. Our products will be safe to make and to use. We will conserve natural resources, and we will continue to invest in a better environment.

We believe that commitment to this mission and to these values will enable the Company to provide a superior return to our shareholders.

A gold medal or nothing at all.

In writing the *Mission* statement, Gillette's operating group decided to focus on product performance rather than organizational structure. This allowed the company to unite behind a single shared goal: . . . **Enhance clear leadership, worldwide** . . . "That's like saying if we were going to send a team to the Olympics, we would choose those events where we had a reasonable chance of winning the gold," Alfred M. Zeien, chairman of the board, told employees. "Because the benefits of being the leader in a consumer products category on a worldwide basis are so great, we have to channel our resources to this direction, and we just don't have the resources to also engage in these other events where there's a possibility we might just win a bronze."

Gillette's **Current Core Categories** include the Gillette line of male and female grooming products such as razors and blades, Right Guard, Dry Idea, and Soft & Dri deodorants and antiperspirants. Then there are stationery products such as Paper Mate, Parker & Waterman pens and Liquid Paper. Rounding out the stable are oral care products like Oral-B toothbrushes and household appliances such as those made by Braun.

"Our mission's philosophy was very much behind our decision to acquire the Parker Pen Company in 1993," says William McMorrow, senior vice president of administration. "Up to that point, our writing instrument business consisted of Paper Mate brand and Waterman. The writing instrument business is very fragmented around the world. We were probably tied for number one at a very low level, say seven or eight percent of that market. The acquisition of Parker probably doubled our positioning in the writing instrument business, so we're in the low teens in terms of our share. By defining our core categories, we have been able to make smarter decisions," he says.

Another way Gillette plans to achieve clear leadership in their core categories is through their new product development program. "It is through new products that we can grow the top lines," says McMorrow. "It is particularly effective in the economic conditions we've had in Europe. The best way to combat that is to lay on a series of demonstrably superior products. Thirty-seven percent of the products sold in 1993 did not exist five years earlier," he says.

The final portion of their mission says . . . **We will also compete in supporting product areas that enhance the company's ability to achieve or hold the leadership position in core categories.** "This was an area that was very controversial," says McMorrow. "It was difficult to deal with employees who are not working in core category companies, such as a toiletry unit, where we knew that the competition was such that we could not become number one. The importance of those businesses was to provide a continuing source of ongoing sales and the ability to absorb some of our manufacturing overhead. That is the way we, frankly, had to be up front with those people and say that was what their mission is," says McMorrow.

Gillette decided to put their *Mission* and *Values* together in one document. The *Values* identify the attitudes and behaviors that employees of the company can expect of each other. "Values are essentials that we hold dear," Zeien told employees. "These are principles. These are a code of conduct. It's very important that we recognize, in setting out a mission, that we do not allow ourselves to think that the mission is so important that we'd give up our values in attempting to achieve it. And that's why it's important that the two be tied together in the same document."

. . . **organizational flexibility** and **personal mobility** are two attributes listed in the *People* section of the *Values* statement. Gillette's "realignment plan," announced in 1993, would fall under this description. Under the plan there will be job additions and reductions over the next two years affecting 2,000 positions, or six percent of the workforce.

The phrase **personal mobility** addresses the worldwide nature of the company. "Eighty percent of our employees, sales, and profits are outside the United States," says McMorrow. "In order for people to be prepared to manage this company in future years, we believe strongly that our people have to be willing to do assignments outside their home country. Of the top forty or fifty executives in the company, approximately eighty percent have done stints outside their own country. Through the *Mission* statement and other things, people understand that their chances of progressing to senior levels of management are enhanced by their willingness to be assigned outside their home country," he says.

Gillette's *Good Citizenship* value mainly addresses legal compliance. In 1993 they set pretty stringent goals in the area of air emissions. "We've set goals in the U.S. and outside the U.S.," says McMorrow. "Doing this around the world presents a challenge. But we feel we have to hold ourselves to the same standards as the United States."

In 1993, Gillette had another great year. Sales were at a record level of $5.41 billion. Net income and earnings per share grew at 15 percent, and, for the eighty-eighth consecutive year, the company paid cash dividends on its common stock. "The strength of Gillette's long-term business results and stock market performance is largely due to our continuing focus on carrying out the Company's mission—to achieve or enhance clear leadership worldwide in the existing or new core consumer product categories in which we choose to operate," Zeien told employees when the mission statement was introduced in 1992.

"This mission statement is the first one the company has done," says McMorrow. This is the first document that was put together and taken around the Gillette world, explained, and got the buy-in of the entire workforce," he says. Gillette has 30,000 employees worldwide, with facilities in twenty-six countries. In 1992 the operating group of Gillette published their mission statement in the annual report and supplemented it with video materials. "About eighty percent of all our employees saw this video and saw an extensive explanation on it by management," says McMorrow. "Every employee was invited to a meeting at which it was explained."

"You'll notice that we haven't called this a vision statement," Zeien had told employees. "I regard a vision as a description of what people like to be. A mission is very different. There are no 'shoulds' or 'woulds.' A mission requires a very clear definition of where you want to go and requires a realizable plan for its achievement," he says.

Goodyear

Our mission is constant improvement in products and services to meet our customers' needs. This is the only means to business success for Goodyear and prosperity for its investors and employees.

Quality Is the Key to Customer Satisfaction

GUIDING PRINCIPLES

CUSTOMER SATISFACTION—Everything we do is directed to the satisfaction of present and future customers. Quality is defined by the current expectations, as well as by future needs and desires of our customers.

PROCESS IMPROVEMENT—Results are achieved through the management of processes. *All* processes—and the resulting products and services—can be improved, forever. The improvements may take the form of revolutionary changes, innovations or the accumulation of many small steps. The improvements may involve such areas as quality, cost, delivery or time.

PEOPLE—We value the commitment, knowledge and creativity of the men and women of Goodyear. Everyone has the ability to contribute to our mission of constant improvement. Cooperation and respect among individuals and departments are fundamental to success.

ACTION BASED ON FACTS—Sound business decisions are based on sound data and rigorous analysis. Facts are reviewed in an atmosphere without blame. Understanding and use of data collection and analysis is vital in all areas.

Total Quality Culture

One of the recurring themes in Goodyear's mission statement and the subsequent *Guiding Principles* is constant improvement: **OUR MISSION is constant improvement in products and services to meet our customers' needs.**

"From a long-term standpoint we need constant improvement," says Mike Burns, vice president of human resources and total quality culture. "As you can see, constant improvement comes up a lot in the *Guiding Principles* as well as in the mission statement. It came out of a process that included a lot of people, but obviously it describes what our chairman, Stanley Gault, is all about. Every associate has the responsibility to continuously improve their work and their relationship with other associates."

All **processes—and the resulting products and services—can be improved, forever. The improvement may take the form of revolutionary changes, innovations or the accumulation of many small steps.** Says Burns: "There is no improvement too small not to be recognized. We concentrate a lot on small improvements. The chairman, for instance, is a stickler about turning off lights. We take it from turning off lights to the introduction of the Aquatred tire in 1991 which revolutionized the industry. All of these are important."

The Aquatred tire has won more engineering and design awards than any other tire. Its tread design drives water to the outside of the tire, giving strong traction and resisting hydroplaning in wet weather. It not only won awards for the product but also for the unique way it was marketed and advertised. *Advertising Age* magazine said Goodyear orchestrated "a classic marketing introduction strategy combining consumer research, a well-timed general media blitz, and a promotional tour."

A unique feature of Goodyear's *Guiding Principles* is the section *Action Based on Facts.* It spells out in detail how decisions will be made in the company. "Historically, companies, including Goodyear, have people who say 'my gut tells me what I have to do.' They call it working from a gut-feeling standpoint. What we're saying in the *Guiding Principles* is that if you go on gut, you'd better have some facts to back it up. We have to do things based on facts. We have to analyze things better. We need to consult the data," says Burns. The part that says **Facts are reviewed in an atmosphere without blame** is crucial to the system. "You can make better decisions based on facts instead of personalities and blaming others," Burns adds. **Sound business decisions are based on sound data and rigorous analysis.** In essence, this section talks about business intelligence, one of the hottest and newest strategic business disciplines in companies today.

Goodyear uses a ten-step process called Systematic Problem Solving. The process is on a chart that is used by all decision makers to take **Action Based on Facts.** The process calls for project selection, team formation, establishing the purpose statement, learning about the problem (current situation), analysis, proposing improvements (improvement plan), results, standardization—assuming that the improvement will become a part of the regular process routine, remaining issues, and lessons learned.

The establishment of Goodyear's *Guiding Principles* grew out of massive changes in the tire industry during the 1980s. For the first time, there was an increasing global market and intense competition. "We had to do a lot of searching about what were our keys to success in the future," says Burns.

"When you look at the 'Q' which is made into the globe [which is on the original mission-statement artwork], that depicts the total quality culture. To make the words truly become what we wanted, we had to decide: What does our mission have to be? Your mission should be your reason to be. That's why we wrote the mission around customers and what they need and how you service them.

"Our leadership, chairman, and top policy makers were looking at where we were going. At that time, in the eighties, there was a big movement around customer service; customer satisfaction was big, and we wanted to make sure what was going on in our company was aligned with that principle. Company leaders were not interested in a one- or two-year program where you emphasize one program then move on to another one.

"We knew *quality* was the one word that had to be part of it. That meant quality in everything we did, not just process, but individual work. The other word we needed was *total*. I shouldn't waste a bit of anything; that's quality. Even scratch paper," says Burns. "We then thought about culture and came up with *Total Quality Culture*. What that meant, however, was that the current culture had to change. Attitudes and behaviors had to change. The thinking process had to change. We had to change our culture," says Burns, "and that led to the development of the *Guiding Principles*.

"The one message that's important is the whole quality culture that we're evolving is geared toward satisfying our shareholders, that we serve our customer with value products and value services, and, third, that we support our associates. These aren't in priority, mind you," Burns says, "because you can't separate associates, customers, and shareholders."

Quality in innovation has always been key to Goodyear's success. The company, founded in 1898, floundered making bicycle and carriage tires until it developed the detachable straight-side auto tire in 1904. It staked its future on that product which was accepted as the industry standard a decade later. The company was built on the name of Charles Goodyear, who died penniless even though he discovered the process of vulcanization which allowed rubber to be turned into flexible, nonbrittle tires capable of withstanding temperature fluctuation and shock. Other Goodyear company innovations include the first American-made synthetic rubber tire and the first nylon cord tire in 1947. Having the first all-season tire—the Tiempo in 1977—was an engineering and marketing bonanza, and having the Goodyear blimp above everyone's head doesn't hurt product recognition either.

The mission statement and *Guiding Principles* are back to back on a pocket card that has been translated into several languages. Says Burns: "I've got mine in a little stand that sits on my desk. A lot of times when I'm having a meeting I'll pick it up and say, 'Hey, it says action based on facts, and I haven't seen enough facts yet.'"

THIS IS HALLMARK

We believe:

That our *products and services* must enrich people's lives
and enhance their relationships.

That *creativity and quality* – in our concepts, products
and services – are essential to our success.

That the *people* of Hallmark are our company's
most valuable resource.

That distinguished *financial performance* is a must,
not as an end in itself, but as a means
to accomplish our broader mission.

That our *private ownership* must be preserved.

The values that guide us are:

Excellence in all we do.

Ethical and moral conduct at all times
and in all our relationships.

Innovation in all areas of our business as a means
of attaining and sustaining leadership.

Corporate social responsibility to Kansas City
and to each community in which we operate.

*These beliefs and values guide our business strategies,
our corporate behavior, and our relationships
with suppliers, customers, communities and each other.*

Maintaining a Standard

The first of the five beliefs in Hallmark's corporate mission statement deals with the goal of their products and services: . . . **our products and services** must enrich people's lives and enhance their relationships. "This belief is central to the nature of our business," said Donald J. Hall, chairman of Hallmark Cards, Inc., and son of the founder, in *Crown*, the company's magazine "Social expression and communications. Enhancing relationships is what we are all about."

. . . *creativity and quality* . . . **are essential to our success,** the next belief, is very dear to Hallmark as well. "The creative process is the very soul of our company," Hall said. Hallmark and Ambassador Cards share the world's largest creative staff—about 700 people. This group generates over 20,000 greeting cards annually. "And we have always stood for quality. These two elements, in tandem, are the constant elements in our chosen formula for success." In 1910, when Joyce Hall created his first postcard in his room at the Kansas City YMCA, his favorite saying was "I'm hell-bent on quality." It set the tone for the company then and today.

The fifth belief, . . . **our *private ownership* must be preserved,** is of utmost importance to Hallmarkers, considering that one-third of the company is owned by the employees. "Our private status is extremely valuable to us," Hall noted in *Crown*. "Remaining private allows us to operate and make business decisions in the long-term best interest of our company: producing products the way they should be made; treating Hallmarkers appropriately, with good, secure employment, and benefiting our communities," he said. "When the news media gets the notion that Hallmark might go public, our employees can be reassured this will not happen, because our beliefs and values state that our private ownership must be preserved."

Not surprisingly, the first Hallmark value is *Excellence* **in all we do.** Hall expanded on this value in *Crown*: "For us excellence is an aspiration, an attitude, a pursuit . . . a way of life. . . . It is the hallmark of this corporation."

Innovation, the third value, has special meaning to Hall. "Innovation at Hallmark is not limited to mechanical or technical advances. Rather, it is a method of approaching our work, with the goal of continuous improvement in mind. In innovation lies our ability to do better tomorrow what we did well today, and to find even better ways beyond that."

Corporate social responsibility, the final value, is an area of pride to Hallmark. A number of things fall under this umbrella, including their legendary *Hallmark Hall of Fame.* They also run a creative workshop for children next to their Kansas City headquarters, called Kaleidoscope, which has a traveling version. The Hallmark Corporate Foundation is focused on children and the elderly and grants funds to supply computers to schools, maintain clinics for children and the elderly, and even weatherize inner-city houses. The Hallmark Employee Volunteer Program matches employees to community needs, resulting in Hallmarkers donating thousands of hours of time volunteering.

As with many other companies, by the late 1980s growth and change fueled the need to codify Hallmark's beliefs and values. "The primary reason [we wrote the mission statement] was that Hallmark was increasing in size and complexity," says Hall. "More employees, more locations, more products. When this happens, you can't assume everyone automatically understands the corporate beliefs and values as they did when the company was smaller. This is particularly true when the beliefs and values have not been written down. We have acquired a number of companies over the years, and their employees need to know what Hallmark stands for," he says. Today Hallmark Cards, including subsidiaries and international operations, has about 21,000 full-time employees and 14,000 part-time employees. They have eight major subsidiaries and annual sales of approximately $3.4 billion. Hallmark has the largest share of the U.S. card market and produces cards in 20 languages and in more than one hundred countries.

"During this time we also were engineering an organizational transformation," says Hall. "We were flattening our structure, developing interdivisional teams, speeding up production, and emphasizing continuous improvement. Beliefs and values are a touchstone in such times of transition—the unchanging foundation on which everything else is built. We wanted to articulate those beliefs and values so that all Hallmarkers could share a common foundation," he says.

Hallmark didn't use any outsiders to write their beliefs and values. "We realized that only a document that uniquely fit our organization would work," says Hall. The team consisted of a few top members of the Hallmark organization, including Hall. "It wasn't difficult," says Hall. "These are the same beliefs and values that have guided our company's business practices from the beginning."

Hallmark's mission statement is entitled *This Is Hallmark*, and is presented in a greeting-card format. The outside cover has the title, with their famous crown logo. When you open the card, the statement is on an insertable card, making it look framed. Every employee receives one of these special greeting cards.

"Our values are the only things that ultimately will protect us from making mistakes that would undermine our reputation, our integrity, and, therefore, our success," says Hall. "Perhaps no other topic is a greater source of both pride and concern for me."

HONDA

HONDA MOTOR CO., LTD.
Company Principle

"Maintaining an international viewpoint, we are dedicated to supplying products of the highest efficiency yet at a reasonable price for worldwide customer satisfaction."

HONDA MOTOR CO., LTD.
Management Policy

☐ Proceed always with ambition and youthfulness.
☐ Respect sound theory, develop fresh ideas and make the most effective use of time.
☐ Enjoy your work, and always brighten your working atmosphere.
☐ Strive constantly for a harmonious flow of work.
☐ Be ever mindful of the value of research and endeavor.

HONDA OF AMERICA MFG., INC.
Operating Priorities

In all areas of manufacturing operations, Honda of America Manufacturing, Inc. observes the following priorities:

1. Safety
2. Quality
3. Production

HONDA OF AMERICA MFG., INC.
Operating Principles

Quality In All Jobs
Learn, Think, Analyze, Evaluate and Improve

Reliable Products
On Time, with Excellence and Consistency

Better Communication
Listen, Ask, and Speak Up

1994 SLOGAN
"Know your customers and exceed their expectations."

7 hours to discuss 23 words

Susan Insley is senior vice president for engine operations at Honda's Anna Engine Plant in Ohio. "The *Company Principle* attracted many of us to come to Honda," says Insley, a nine-year employee. "As senior managers we take the responsibility to teach it, share it, and live it."

"**Maintaining an international viewpoint** . . ." "When you work in a factory, one can tend to get tunnel vision. We want our associates to think more broadly than just their department or their plant. The Anna plant produces twenty-seven percent of the Honda engines and drivetrains of Honda's worldwide output. We exported about forty-five thousand automobiles last year. It is crucial for everyone to understand the worldwide viewpoint," says Insley. Executive Vice President for Honda of America Manufacturing Scott Whitlock says, " '**Maintaining an international viewpoint**' means that Honda strives to be competitive around the world. Honda of America was the first manufacturer to export five percent of product; in 1994 we'll be the first to export fifteen percent, mostly to Europe."

"Every country has different safety and environmental standards for automobiles," says Insley. "Most U.S. automakers certify their export vehicles outside the U.S. We export to twenty-nine countries. It's more time consuming and more costly to certify in each country, so Honda associates certify them in our plants right here. In 1989 we were the first U.S. manufacturer to produce right- and left-hand-steer cars in the same production line. Our exports represent six weeks worth of work to us right now." It's part of maintaining an international viewpoint. "Even our bonus sharing program is based on Honda's worldwide pretax profits," says Insley.

. . . **we are dedicated** . . . "Dedication takes many forms and takes a lot of effort," says Insley. "We ask our associates to think about dedication in relationship to their job, to think about their attitude. It seems hard to talk with a straight face about dedication in a manufacturing job," says Whitlock. "But we have high levels of dedication."

Whitlock talks about the concept of the "three joys." "The three joys are the foundation for the company principle," says Whitlock. The three joys are using or consuming a product, selling the product, and producing or manufacturing the product. The three joys and the *Company Principle* were created by the founders of the company, Messrs. Honda and Fujisawa. "They were in business together," says Whitlock. "They spent a lot of time talking about company philosophy. Out of these talks came the three joys and the *Company Principle*."

. . . **to supplying products of the highest efficiency yet at a reasonable price** . . . "This is a big challenge," says Insley. "We have to design and develop, manufacture, sell, and service the highest efficiency product that will delight and please the customers—that they'll be proud to own. We have to be careful that the price is one the customer deems reasonable. That creates a big burden on production not to say no to research and development."

To handle this dilemma and serve their *Company Principle*, Honda of America developed a system called S.E.D.: sales, engineering, and development. "All three must be involved from the beginning," says Insley. "An example of this system is the 1994 model Accord. It's better designed and better engineered—at a competitive cost. That team worked to create this product. Everything was kept in balance—highest efficiency, reasonable price. There were a number of improvements and no increase in price. We have a very clear engineering-based strategy. Mr. Honda was an engineer."

. . . **worldwide customer satisfaction.** Insley tells the associates to think about "who is my customer?" "If you're on the production line, who's the next person affected? That's your customer too. At Anna Engine we have four immediate customers—the Marysville Auto Plant, the Marysville Motorcycle Plant, the East Liberty Auto Plant and the Honda of Canada Plant." But the outside customer is equally important. Insley relates a story told to her at a meeting by fellow associate Steve Powell. "He was the manager of the paint department in Marysville. The paint department was being revamped and there were enormous concerns about the quality of the painting because of the dust. We had many complaints from dealers. The plant manager, who happened to be Scott Whitlock at the time, got a call from a dealer in Oklahoma who had a very angry customer. The customer said the paint job was so bad that he didn't want the car.

Scott passed along the information to Steve and Steve flew to Oklahoma to see the customer and the zone representative. Steve took one look at the car and thought about their principle—the part about **worldwide customer satisfaction.** Steve told the dealer to give the man a new car." Insley continues. "This story illustrates that even nine years ago, when this happened, a new manager understood what customer satisfaction is all about."

Senior executives at Honda of America Manufacturing teach a course on their *Company Principle.* The course lasts seven hours. The *Company Principle* is 23 words long. Insley teaches the class once a month on the basic Honda philosophies with fifteen associates per class. Every Tuesday, Insley meets with five new Honda associates. They talk about the *Company Principle.* They talk about the international-viewpoint part or dedication or customer service. Then she follows up with each group after two months and she talks about a different part of the *Principle* and how they can use it everyday in their jobs.

The *Principle* is on the walls of all meeting rooms and in all the plants. "It's not the Holy Grail," says Insley, "but it is our basic foundation."

IBM

Principles

- The marketplace is the driving force behind everything that we do.
- At our core, we are a technology company with an overriding commitment to quality.
- Our primary measures of success are customer satisfaction and shareholder value.
- We operate as an entrepreneurial organization with a minimum of bureaucracy and a never-ending focus on productivity.
- We never lose sight of our strategic vision.
- We think and act with a sense of urgency.
- Outstanding, dedicated people make it all happen, particularly when they work together as a team.
- We are sensitive to the needs of all employees and to the communities in which we operate.

IBM'S BASIC BELIEFS

I. Respect for the Individual.

II. The Best Customer Service of any Company in the World.

III. The Pursuit of All Tasks with the Idea That They Can Be Accomplished in a Superior Fashion.

Pay attention to the marketplace— and not a moment too soon.

Once honored by other corporations for its esprit de corps and commitment to excellence, IBM has become a prime abject example of a company that had to change its very culture if it was to survive.

The first *Principle* of IBM's mission statement is the most important: **The marketplace is the driving force behind everything we do.** Because of its great size and position, IBM was used to telling customers what they needed instead of customers telling IBM what they wanted. "We spent too little time thinking about the customer," says Pat McCracken, director of internal communication. Chairman Lou Gerstner acknowledged this problem in his letter to investors in the 1993 annual report. In discussing IBM's problems, he wrote: "At the heart of this turmoil is one simple fact: IBM failed to keep pace with significant change in the industry." Most important, customers were changing to PCs and IBM wasn't paying attention.

Also crucial is the *Principle* that deals with urgency: **We think and act with a sense of urgency.** "It's part of how we try to operate," says McCracken. "For one thing, we have a sense of urgency to get information to employees before they read it in the media." IBM used to be so slow and bureaucratic that employees often read about the latest company decision in newspaper articles and trade journals instead of hearing it from internal sources.

"We're also starting to see a sense of urgency in how decisions are made, like in reducing cycle times so we can get products to market more quickly. We used to do a lot of task-force work. Now we don't. We often came up with great technology, but we let our competitors beat us to the market with it."

Great technology will always be an important factor according to the *Principles:* **At our core, we are a technology company with an overriding commitment to quality.** IBM has always had some of the world's best researchers, but their marching orders are different under the new *Principles*. "Our research division, which used to be focused on pure research and long-term objectives, is now more focused on product," says McCracken.

Interestingly, if you look at *IBM's Basic Beliefs* written in 1962 by Tom Watson, Jr., son of the company's founder, you see that people come first—**Respect for the Individual.** However in Gerstner's *Principles*, employees are mentioned last. Clearly, IBM's new aim is survival and not employee comfort, although McCracken dismisses this criticism as a bit severe. "People are still our foundation. It's our competitive advantage. Lou Gerstner likes to think that mentioning people is at the bottom, because it holds the other principles up."

Are the *Principles* working? "It's evolving. I wouldn't say the whole company has changed overnight. Absolutely not, but it's getting there. It's going to mean people getting comfortable with it. What does it mean in how I do things in my day-to-day job."

In 1992 Big Blue was in trouble. IBM stock—once so solid that it was for decades dubbed the "stock for widows and orphans"—was going into freefall. The computer giant was losing money to the tune of $5 billion, with no end in sight.

What could have gone wrong with this rock-solid company that single-handedly brought the world into the computer age? Now, looking back, it's almost too simple. IBM, like many other giants, was too slow-moving to keep pace with the fast world it had helped create. While the rest of its competitors had seen the coming of the personal computer, IBM decided to stick with what it knew best—large mainframe computers. In addition, the company, once recognized for its corporate élan and precision, was now too bulky and bureaucratic to compete in a world where it had to deal with faster-moving, smaller, unencumbered competitors.

In 1993 IBM's board of directors recruited Lou Gerstner, formerly of RJR Nabisco and American Express Travel, to help bring it out of its morass. One of the first things he did was thin the ranks, something unthinkable for a company that had prided itself on a no-layoff policy. Among his other initiatives, the man who spent twenty years at consultancy McKinsey & Co. helping other companies out of similar messes, also decided to change the company culture. If IBM was to survive, it would have to change the way it thought about itself and the world around it.

"IBM had been very bureaucratic, very rule driven," says Mc-Cracken. "We had guidelines for everything. It had gotten a little bit out of control. We were caught up in our internal plumbing. We spent too much time and energy on internal bureaucratic kinds of things instead of the customer."

Gerstner decided that IBM would no longer be a company based on rules. Instead, it would be run by principles. "This way you don't have to run to the rule book every time you make a decision. If you run the company based on principles, then you'll always do the right thing," says McCracken.

At the end of 1993 (losses for the year reached $8 billion) Gerstner penned the *IBM Principles*, which McCracken introduced to the rank and file. "We first mentioned it in our employee newspaper. We had a special edition of *Think* magazine (long the company motto) and we called it *Think Twice*. We're trying to lighten things up a little at IBM," says McCracken of the title of the special edition. "It also means that it's something we want people to reflect on. *Think Twice* should last a little longer than *Think*." Writing in *Think Twice*, Gerstner told IBMers: "We don't need rule books to tell people what to do. We have only to tell them: 'Manage whatever you do against this set of principles and we will trust your judgment.' "

Unlike many other executives who write principles and send them out for review, Gerstner stuck with what he said. It's exactly as he wrote them. "IBM used to be consensus driven," says McCracken, "but Lou is big on making decisions: implement and execute. We were careful not to make this a PR campaign. We didn't want to get rhetoric ahead of reality, which often happens when you try to get everybody to know something without really understanding it. We are introducing this slowly. We want all managers worldwide to read and understand what it really means. We've been careful not to do buttons and posters, plus we didn't want to spend a lot of money." McCracken says that managers in the field were on such tight budgets that she had to reassure them that funds to publicize the *Principles* would come out of her corporate budget and not their budgets.

Adds McCracken: "Lou's using the *Principles* to reshape the company. This is Gerstner's dream, one step at a time."

19

INTEL CO

OUR MISSION

*Do a great job for our customers,
employees and stockholders by
being the preeminent building block
supplier to the computing industry.*

OUR VALUES

CUSTOMER ORIENTATION:

**Partnerships with our customers
and suppliers are essential to our
mutual success.**

We strive to:
- Listen to our customers.
- Communicate mutual intentions
  and expectations.
- Deliver innovative and competitive
  products and services.
- Make it easy to work with us.
- Serve our customers through
  partnerships with our suppliers.

RESULTS ORIENTATION:

We are results oriented.

We strive to:
- Set challenging goals.
- Execute flawlessly.
- Focus on output.
- Assume responsibility.
- Confront and solve problems.

DISCIPLINE:

**The complexity of our work and
tough business environment demands
a high degree of self discipline
and cooperation.**

We strive to:
- Properly plan, fund and staff projects.
- Pay attention to detail.
- Clearly communicate intentions
  and expectations.
- Make and meet commitments.
- Conduct business with uncompromising
  integrity and professionalism.

intel.

9 4
R P O R A T I O N

1. Strengthen our number one position in the microprocessor market segment.

- Make the Pentium™ processor ramp the fastest in history.
- Double system performance at every price point.
- Fight off architecture and imitator challenges.
- Capitalize on growing PC consumption in Asia.
- Extend the Intel architecture to mobile companions.
- Ensure 90% of major new PC introductions are Intel Verified.

2. Make the PC THE ubiquitous interactive device.

- Lead in LAN products and Smart Network Services.
- Successfully deliver personal conferencing products to the PC space.
- Make the PC accepted as the interactive information device in the home.
- Be #1 in PC connectivity devices (desktop and mobile).
- Drive major growth in the Intel386™ CPU embedded market.

3. Do the right things right.

- Solve any problems which might limit Pentium processor **platform** growth.
- Show leadership in component and system time-to-market.
- Build 2x upside capability into our planning, scheduling and delivery systems.
- Double the size of our standard semiconductor business by 1995.
- Continuously redeploy people and assets to projects with greater value added.
- Elevate our customer support capability to match our brand image.

GREAT PLACE TO WORK:

A productive and challenging work environment is key to our success.

We strive to:
- Respect and trust each other.
- Be open and direct.
- Work as a team.
- Maintain a safe workplace.
- Recognize and reward accomplishments.
- Be an asset to the community.
- Have fun!

QUALITY:

Our business requires continuous improvement of our performance to our Mission and Values.

We strive to:
- Set challenging and competitive goals.
- Do the right things right.
- Continuously learn, develop and improve.
- Take pride in our work.

RISK TAKING:

To succeed we must maintain our innovative environment.

We strive to:
- Embrace change.
- Challenge the status quo.
- Listen to all ideas and viewpoints.
- Encourage and reward informed risk taking.
- Learn from our successes and mistakes.

Printed in U.S.A./1293/23k/Bofors/BA
Order number: 241930-001
Printed on recycled paper
©1994 Intel Corporation

Take risks. Have fun. Produce results.

Intel's mission statement, values, and objectives are curiously like the computer chips that the company manufactures. The basic concept stays the same, but some parts are upgraded and made more powerful on a regular basis. In 1994 the statement featured the Intel inside logo, which the company now places on computers that use the Intel microprocessor chip. It's a bold move for a company that has kept a low profile for years.

Our Mission and *Our Values* are sections that stay pretty much the same year after year. *Our Objectives* changes depending upon the company's focus. "The statements have been around in published form around six or seven years," says Kirby Dyess, vice president of human resources. "The challenge is to swap last year's objectives with this year's objectives."

One of the company's *Values* reflects this higher profile attitude: **Make it easy to work with us.** Says Dyess: "This is a goal related to our customers. We need to understand what our customers want, and we've made it easier to contact us. I never thought I'd see the day when we had 800 numbers that allow customers to contact us directly. We were relatively invisible. Now customers want to know what we're doing and how we're doing it. The personal-computer customer is much more sophisticated than years ago. People want to know where the chip is going."

The chip in question is Intel's latest high-speed product known as the Pentium. The Pentium processor chip is the fastest chip available to commercial PC users. After years of increasing speed with their 286, 386, and 486 chips (and incremental steps for each one), Intel decided to stop the numbers and give it a name. Apparently, it was easier to copyright a name and it also gave the chip better customer recognition.

The *Objectives* for 1994 set aggressive goals for the new chip, including **Make the Pentium™ processor ramp the fastest in history.** The goals also call for fighting challengers who want to imitate the chip, and the loftiest goal of all: **Ensure 90% of major new PC introductions are Intel Verified,** that is, use the Intel chip.

Intel is not a traditional company and breaks some of the more traditional rules of business. One difference is their attitude about redeployment. The objectives make it quite clear that Intel can **continuously redeploy people and assets to projects with greater value added.** In other words, if we need you over there, then you work over there.

"We move people around on a regular basis, and that can be a painful process," says Dyess. "If I see myself as a human resources professional but we find ourselves in a position where there aren't enough jobs in human resources, then I've got to start to see myself as a financial analyst or a supervisor in a wafer fabrication organization or something like that. When you look at the value of transferring around the company, though, and the knowledge base that is transferred, it's very beneficial. We get a large payback in that respect."

Another traditional rule that Intel has broken is about risk taking. Although many companies say they encourage risk taking, Intel actually rewards it and at the same time doesn't punish mistakes.

Risk taking is so crucial to Intel that the *Values* has an entire section devoted to it. The company strives to: **Embrace change . . . Challenge the status quo . . . Listen to all ideas and viewpoints . . . Encourage and reward informed risk taking . . . Learn from our successes and mistakes.**

"We don't punish someone for taking an informed risk and failing," says Dyess. "We rarely see people here today and gone tomorrow because they've taken a risk and failed. In fact, they're often given a chance to do something similar again, because they've probably learned a lot from the experience. People do learn from their failures, sometimes more than from their successes. We encourage it by not punishing it and also by recognizing and rewarding it when it's successful." According to Dyess, the most valued reward at Intel is when your manager does something special just for you—individualized rewards.

The risk-taking attitude goes hand in hand with one of the other company tenets—being results oriented. Dyess says that internal surveys show that workers continue to see Intel's main personality as one of achieving specific results. Reading the *Objectives*, you see the short-term results set for the company, but in *Our Values*, workers strive to **Execute flawlessly . . . Focus on output . . . Assume responsibility**. "People here assume the responsibility and take it forward," says Dyess. "We encourage employees to be stockholders. It helps them look at things and assume responsibility from a different perspective."

One of the company's values is to make Intel a **Great Place to Work.** To that end is the statement **Have fun!** This may seem like a contradiction because Intel is not an easy place to work. It's intense. In fact, some in the industry tell the story that the most frequently heard phrase at Intel is "Only the paranoid survive." It's a place for people who like to work hard under grueling deadlines and demanding goals. In return, however, people at the company also play hard, and they don't take themselves too seriously. In addition, titles are not taken to heart either. There are no executive perks, no special parking spaces, and everyone has the same cubicles.

Every year, the April Fool's edition of *Intel Leads*, the firm's internal publication, pokes fun at everything and everyone at Intel no matter what their position. To an outsider, this ridicule may seem like disrespect for authority, but not at Intel. Everyone is fair game, and the jokes can cut deep. You have to have thick skin to work at Intel.

"We work very hard. We play very hard. There needs to be a time to work and release," says Dyess. "Sometimes there's a sense of 'I'm going to do something crazy.'" It's not unusual for teams who just completed an exhausting project to let themselves go by donning helmets and going to a race track to push cars as hard as they've pushed themselves.

Ultimately, however, workers are not judged by how they compete against each other but by how they perform against the *Our Values*— what the company says is important.

"That goes for everyone all the way up the executive office who gets a review from their subordinates on how they're modeling the values," says Dyess.

OUR CREDO

We believe our first responsibility is to the doctors, nurses and patients,
to mothers and fathers and all others who use our products and services.
In meeting their needs everything we do must be of high quality.
We must constantly strive to reduce our costs
in order to maintain reasonable prices.
Customers' orders must be serviced promptly and accurately.
Our suppliers and distributors must have an opportunity
to make a fair profit.

We are responsible to our employees,
the men and women who work with us throughout the world.
Everyone must be considered as an individual.
We must respect their dignity and recognize their merit.
They must have a sense of security in their jobs.
Compensation must be fair and adequate,
and working conditions clean, orderly and safe.
We must be mindful of ways to help our employees fulfill
their family responsibilities.
Employees must feel free to make suggestions and complaints.
There must be equal opportunity for employment, development
and advancement for those qualified.
We must provide competent management,
and their actions must be just and ethical.

We are responsible to the communities in which we live and work
and to the world community as well.
We must be good citizens — support good works and charities
and bear our fair share of taxes.
We must encourage civic improvements and better health and education.
We must maintain in good order
the property we are privileged to use,
protecting the environment and natural resources.

Our final responsibility is to our stockholders.
Business must make a sound profit.
We must experiment with new ideas.
Research must be carried on, innovative programs developed
and mistakes paid for.
New equipment must be purchased, new facilities provided
and new products launched.
Reserves must be created to provide for adverse times.
When we operate according to these principles,
the stockholders should realize a fair return.

Johnson & Johnson

It got them through the Tylenol poisoning crisis.

"Companies usually don't get a test of this type to ascertain the importance of a business philosophy, but having the *Credo* helped Johnson & Johnson employees unconsciously take the steps necessary to do the right thing," Robert Kniffen, vice president of corporate relations, says.

Johnson & Johnson's true test of doing the right thing occurred in 1982 during the Tylenol tamperings. Kniffin, who was at the company then, tells the story: "In 1982, when the poisoning occurred in Chicago, where someone put cyanide poison in the capsules, we had an unprecedented situation and had to invent ways of dealing with it. For example, that day the chairman sent me and someone from the law department to Pennsylvania, where the product was made [McNeil Consumer]. I spent the next ten days there dealing with the media, and we had to deal with them the best we could. Multiply that with the phone calls we got from consumers, from doctors, from hospitals, and from law enforcement agencies. We didn't know what happened, whether something had happened in the plant or outside. To know beyond a shadow of a doubt took weeks.

"I was in the president's office [at McNeil Consumer] and he had asked the vice president of finance to compute what it would cost to recall all of the capsules in the United States. This guy came back and said he calculated that it would be seventy-five million dollars. And then he said, 'But we don't have seventy-five million dollars,' meaning McNeil Consumer. Then there was a pause and another guy said, 'But how can we *not* do this, because there might be another bottle on the shelf, and if we don't get them back, someone might die.' It was not an instance where someone said, 'Let's consult the *Credo* and think through this problem, starting with what's our responsibility to the consumer, but rather it was a way of looking at the world, at business, and at the decisions. The *Credo* structures the way you think about things. When all that was done and the dust had settled, we reached the conclusion that those hundreds of individual decisions were right decisions. They sprang from some common way of looking at the world, which in retrospect was the *Credo*."

At the time, Tylenol was the company's largest single moneymaker. During the incident, their market share of the analgesic market dropped from 37 percent to 7 percent within weeks and the company's share price dropped 10 percent. In five months a new tamperproof Tylenol was back on the shelves, and it had regained 70 percent of its previous market share. Within three years its total market share was reached.

"The premise of the document [*Our Credo*] was that if you order your priorities, most of the time it will work out. There are conflicts, of course. It was not in the stockholders' interest to take a $50 million after-tax write off. Nobody ever complained about that, which is interesting. It all seems clear in retrospect, but during those first few days nothing was clear. I was convinced we were going to lose that brand. The decision was made to recall the capsules altogether. As a result of that, we did find three bottles on the shelves in Chicago that were poisoned," says Kniffen.

Then Chairman James Burke was quoted at the time: "After the crisis was over we realized that no meeting had been called to make the first critical decision. Everyone of us knew what we had to do. We had the *Credo* to guide us."

Johnson & Johnson is one of those great American corporate classics. Started in 1886 by the three Johnson brothers with fourteen employees in New Brunswick, New Jersey, Johnson & Johnson today has 82,000 employees worldwide and $14 billion in sales. Johnson & Johnson has produced some of the world's most well-known brands, including Johnson's Baby Powder, which was introduced in 1893; Band-Aids, introduced in 1920; and Tylenol, in 1960.

Johnson & Johnson's *Our Credo* is their corporate mission statement and guiding philosophy. It was written by General Robert Wood Johnson more than fifty years ago. *Our Credo* covers four main areas of responsibility: customers, employees, communities, and shareholders.

"For its time, it was extremely forward looking and visionary," says

Robert Kniffin. "It was challenged by the management in the mid-seventies, when the chairman decided if it was going to hang on walls and be on desks in offices that it should not just be a token or symbol, but should be an article of faith," he says.

"He convened a couple of meetings with top management and challenged them with provocative questions about the conflicting tenets of the *Credo*. For example, an inefficient plant that you've had for many years. If you close it, what happens to the community; what about your obligation to employees? Or, what do you do with a batch of product that is fine but the labels are on crooked? People argued with considerable emotion about such things, with the object of asking whether this document was necessary and desirable, and if so, should it be modernized or changed. Out of that came some changes. That *Credo* challenge process continues right up until this day, and has resulted in some further changes in the text, but remarkably few, in my opinion," he says.

"We are going through a period of enormous change, facing all kinds of challenges—from customers, from competitors, from government," Chairman and Chief Executive Officer Ralph Larsen had told employees. "When you go through that kind of stressful challenge, you've got to be rooted in a set of fundamental beliefs. When we talk to our constituencies—hospitals, retailers, suppliers, government regulators, even competitors—they presume that we are going to do the right thing and act honorably," Larsen noted.

You'll find the *Credo* part of the vocabulary at Johnson & Johnson, from developing "*Credo*-based" leaders to "*Credo* challenge meetings" to "*Credo* surveys." *Credo* challenge meetings, begun in 1976, continue today at J&J. About 25 people attend each session and the session deals with the results of the *Credo* survey, which is done on a three-year cycle. The *Credo* survey is a series of more than a hundred questions that give each employee (anonymously) the chance to rate how well the company is living up to the tenets of the *Credo*. People in the challenge sessions are asked to reflect on why some areas receive higher scores than others and how those scores tie into the implementation of the values outlined in the credo.

Could you work for Johnson & Johnson? You have to believe in the *Credo* to climb the corporate ladder. As Ralph Larsen told employees: "While it is possible to succeed in Johnson & Johnson over the short term without a true commitment to the credo, . . . you will not do well over the long term. You have to believe in *Our Credo* and practice it to be able to finish your career with Johnson & Johnson."

MARY KAY COSMETICS INC.

"All you send into the lives of others comes back into your own."

– Mary Kay Ash
Chairman Emeritus

 MARY KAY

THE MARY KAY VISION

- To be preeminent in the manufacturing, distribution, and marketing of personal care products through our independent sales force.

- To provide our sales force an unparalleled opportunity for financial independence, career achievement, and personal fulfillment.

- To achieve total customer satisfaction worldwide by focusing on quality, value, convenience, innovation, and personal service.

— Richard C. Bartlett, Vice Chairman
Mary Kay Corporation

MARY KAY – THE LEARNING ORGANIZATION

We believe:

INTEGRITY and fairness guides every business decision, using the Golden Rule and go-give spirit as heartfelt principles.

SERVICE should be thoughtful, prompt, and proactive to provide convenience with a personal touch.

QUALITY in our products and services is of the utmost importance in delivering value and satisfaction to our customers.

ENTHUSIASM encourages a can-do, positive attitude, and provides laughter and inspiration as we work to achieve our goals.

PRAISE encourages everyone to grow and reach their full potential.

TEAMWORK enhances performance because each individual contributes to the success of the organization when he or she is needed and appreciated by others.

LEADERSHIP among our sales force and employees is encouraged and recognized because effective leaders will help us achieve long-term success.

PRIORITIES lead to balanced lives, with God, family, and career in harmony.

**The lives of everyone who comes in contact with our Company
— employees, sales force, customers, and vendors —
should be enhanced by their association with us.**

♻ Printed on recycled paper with soybean oil-based ink.   Printed in U.S.A. C93

Focus on the people who make the product.

Preeminence is a very important concept to Richard C. Bartlett, vice chairman, and to the Mary Kay Corporation. He incorporated it into the mission statement, *The Mary Kay Vision*, in 1987, around the time he became president of the company. "To me a sense of pride on the part of the employees and executives involved is a critical part of the vision," he says. "Having a sense of pride in the sales organization and in the employees was the first critical thing I addressed as president. I didn't want to put the biggest or the best, because a mission statement has to be doable and believable. If you use the words '**To be preeminent**,' you'd better be prepared to back it up. It's a journey, not a destination."

The order of the words following "**To be preeminent**" was a big challenge for Bartlett. "The executives really challenged putting *manufacturing* first [before distribution and marketing]. But I felt this gives me a chance to praise the employees in manufacturing, an often-overlooked segment of the company, especially in a vertical organization. It enables me to bring those employees right into the picture. As a result, our manufacturing division is the best quantitatively. We are the most efficient producers of fine cosmetics on earth."

The Mary Kay distribution section is also a source of pride for Bartlett. "We have been benchmarked by *Industry Week*, along with Hershey and L. L. Bean, and ranked the three best distribution companies in America. We're being benchmarked locally by Texas Instruments, which our distribution people love. They really do believe they're the best," he says.

Putting **personal care products** in the mission statement gives the Mary Kay people a focus, says Bartlett. Their independent sales force is also "a source of tremendous comfort and power in our organization," he says. "You cannot afford to erode loyalty. We are what we believe in. Our top independent salespeople make a million dollars annually. The top recognition group all make more than the President of the United

States. They can literally earn what they want to earn. The whole program is structured for advancement."

The concept of **personal fulfillment** is critical to the success of the Mary Kay salespeople. "These are powerful words to us," says Bartlett. "So many of our people in the sales organization achieve self-confidence out there by helping and teaching others. I call it 'a paycheck of the heart.' I can do something today to help someone else achieve something."

Achieving **total customer satisfaction** might be an unreachable goal, admits Bartlett. "To have it in your *Vision* keeps you on your feet. If not, we have a one-hundred-percent return guarantee—no questions asked. Thank heaven it doesn't happen too often, less than one percent," he says.

The word **value** is a big one for Bartlett. "Price factors into it, but value is the whole package to me. Value means really building a good product, testing it against the competition, and then pricing it in a way that beats the competition for better value."

In their core values, under priorities, God is mentioned. **Priorities lead to balanced lives, with God, family, and career in harmony.** "God is in there because of Mary Kay Ash, pure and simple," says Bartlett. "We have a little philosophical difference about this, but her name is on the building. I prefer the word 'faith.' When I go over this verbally, I use faith, especially when I'm in a different culture.

"I've been over the *Vision* statement face-to-face with almost ten thousand employees," he says. "I start every orientation for every new corporate employee and every independent salesperson who has been promoted to a leadership position with the vision. When we have surveyed those people, along with our employee feedback surveys, we have almost one hundred percent awareness that we have a vision statement, and almost everyone knows what it is about."

Mary Kay Ash started her company in 1963 with $5,000. She had been in direct sales for years and dreamed of a company based on the Golden Rule and a place where women could have unlimited opportunities. Today Mary Kay Cosmetics has more than 325,000 independent sales consultants worldwide and sells to 20 million customers. And those pink Cadillacs you've heard about? More than 7,000 women are driving Mary Kay Cadillacs or other Mary Kay career cars.

The Mary Kay Corporation bought themselves off the New York Stock Exchange in 1985 in a management-led leveraged buyout. "At that time the company was disintegrating into functional silos. We had fiefdoms that would not work together. In 1986 the company continued to downward slide, and we incurred a tremendous amount of debt as a result of the LBO. I felt it imperative that we have some unifying mission," says Bartlett.

The Mary Kay Corporation has done well after their LBO in the late eighties, especially with the *Vision* to guide them. "I believe every company should be focused, fast, flexible, and fun," says Bartlett. "The mission statement helps you be focused."

Kellogg
Our Mission

Kellogg is a global company committed to building long-term growth in volume and profit and to enhancing its worldwide leadership position by providing nutritious food products of superior value.

OUR WORKING ENVIRONMENT

The challenge of an increasingly competitive global marketplace requires an environment within our Company which encourages personal initiative and enables Kellogg people to contribute to their full potential. This environment must promote a free exchange of information, the generation of new ideas, and the continued accumulation of knowledge.

To meet this challenge, we will:

- Exhibit a high level of personal integrity and fairness which respects the individual and our cultural diversity.
- Demonstrate leadership which encourages teamwork, open communication, and mutual trust.
- Approach our work with a focus on results, a sense of urgency, and a healthy dissatisfaction with the status quo.

OUR SHARED VALUES

- Profit and Growth
- People
- Consumer Satisfaction and Quality

- Integrity and Ethics
- Social Responsibility

PROFIT AND GROWTH

Profitable growth is our primary purpose. We are committed to consistent, long-term growth in earnings and to superior returns for our shareholders. We want to be, and be recognized as, a growth Company.

To meet this commitment, we will:

- Grow and expand our core businesses.
- Strengthen our global leadership in ready-to-eat cereal.
- Provide nutritious products of superior quality and value.
- Excel in the introduction of products that meet consumer needs.
- Consider acquisition opportunities consistent with our growth and profit objectives.

PEOPLE

Kellogg people are our Company's greatest competitive advantage. Each and every individual will be given the opportunity to contribute to and share in the Company's success. We are committed to helping Kellogg people reach their full potential and to recognizing their achievements.

To meet this commitment, we will:

- Attract, select, and retain top quality people.
- Provide training, development, and growth opportunities.
- Promote from within whenever possible.
- Provide an environment in which people can excel based on shared values, open communications, and shared learning.
- Recognize achievement and reward performance.

- Provide equal opportunity and respect the cultural diversity of Kellogg people.

CONSUMER SATISFACTION AND QUALITY

The consumer is the ultimate judge of our success. Kellogg people, together with our suppliers and trade partners, will provide consumers with products and services of superior value. We are committed to excellence in everything we do.

To meet this commitment, we will:

- Strive for excellence as defined by our internal and external customers.
- Pursue partnerships with our customers, suppliers, and Kellogg people to achieve common goals.
- Promote continuous and measurable improvement to increase our competitive advantage and leadership position.
- Build responsibility for quality into every function in our organization.

INTEGRITY AND ETHICS

Integrity is the cornerstone of our business practice. We will conduct our affairs in a manner consistent with the highest ethical standards.

To meet this commitment, we will:

- Engage in fair and honest business practices.
- Show respect for each other, our consumers, customers, suppliers, shareholders, and the communities in which we operate.
- Communicate in an honest, factual, and accurate manner.

SOCIAL RESPONSIBILITY

Social responsibility is an integral part of our heritage. We are committed to be, and be recognized as, an economic, intellectual, and social asset in each community, region, and country in which we operate.

To meet this commitment, we will:

- Produce quality products and market them in a responsible manner.
- Encourage Kellogg people to participate in community programs and invest company resources, human and financial, in organizations that benefit the people in our communities.
- Ensure our facilities, working environments, and employment practices reflect good citizenship.
- Conduct our business in a manner which protects the environment and demonstrates good stewardship of our world's natural resources.

"A healthy dissatisfaction with the status quo."

What? The people who give us Kellogg's Corn Flakes are dissatisfied?

. . . we will: **Approach our work with a focus on results, a sense of urgency, and a healthy dissatisfaction with the status quo.**

"We probably use that [phrase] more than any other," says Arnold Langbo, chairman and CEO of the Kellogg Company. "We have been for a long time a very successful company, but success can be your worst enemy. We want to be careful that we don't become overconfident. Some people use the word *arrogant*. Successful as we've been, we never want to be satisfied. We always want to approach each day with a healthy dissatisfaction of the status quo."

Another important aim of the company's philosophy is to keep the company focused. Despite its size and revenues (over $6 billion in 1992), it refused to follow the trend toward diversification. "We have never diversified beyond our mission statement which says **providing nutritious food products.** Instead," says Langbo, "we've been growing our business around the world. That's been our form of diversification —geographic diversification."

Kellogg's has a presence in 160 countries and is perhaps second only to Coca-Cola in global reach. The company has opened facilities in China, India, and will soon serve the nations of the former Soviet Union through facilities in Latvia. "Still," says Langbo, "we're fairly narrow in what we make and sell." The company makes such products as Raisin Bran, Mini-Wheats, Nutri-Grain, Corn Pops, Product 19, Special K, and tens more breakfast cereals. It produces a few other food products, including Eggos, Nutri-Grain Cereal Bars, and Mrs. Smith's frozen desserts. Echoes Joseph Stewart, senior vice president of corporate affairs: "There's no reason to diversify. There's nothing out there that has the same potential as growing our business geographically."

Langbo counters detractors who charge that the cereal business is too concentrated (Kellogg has almost 40 percent of the U.S. market and about 50 percent of the global market) and that cereals are too expensive. "Consumers don't agree with the critics that our products are too expensive. Consumers are taking these products at about three percent annual growth," says Langbo. "The consumer is the ultimate judge of our success. We say so in those very words in our mission statement, and the consumer is rewarding us with a lot more volume."

Langbo, who has been with Kellogg's for 37 years, says that what founder William Kellogg said in the 1920s, "We are a company of dedicated people providing quality products for a healthier world," is similar to what is in the current mission statement. In 1981, however, it was felt that it should be committed to words. At that time the company adopted four organizational goals: profit and growth, investment in people, quality in everything, and social responsibility. In 1986 a group of managers reaffirmed these goals.

However, in 1992 (Langbo became chairman in 1991) 38 top managers from all over the world in all disciplines met and revised the philosophy still further. They worked for a whole week, starting on a Sunday, to get the document together. "It went slowly," Langbo remembers, "but around Thursday it started to blossom. It didn't come down by edict from the chairman's office but has the ownership of all key Kellogg management from around the world with their employees in mind."

One addition was a section called *Integrity and Ethics*. Says Langbo: "We put it in because of the new global structure of the company. We were pushing responsibility out into the field and not at Battle Creek." Increased field responsibility would improve quality and timing of decisions. "We wanted to make a strong statement for everyone everywhere. We wanted everyone to be absolutely clear on what was expected of them."

As if telling people about the importance of integrity and ethics was not enough, the philosophy book shows them as well. There's a picture of a lone corn flake chip standing on end with the caption: "A reputation is a very fragile thing."

A section on cultural diversity was also added to the philosophy during the 1992 meeting. "We wanted to take the Kellogg culture all over the world, but the Kellogg company of India, for example, has to assimilate into the Indian culture as well as be part of the Kellogg culture," says Langbo. "They have to come together, and you do that by respecting various cultural differences."

The company's philosophy booklet has been translated into 15 languages. Says Stewart: "I don't want to sound overreligious about it, but no matter where you go, the book feels the same; it looks the same; the only thing that's different is the language it's written in. This philosophy has to be exact all over the Kellogg world. Not one word can be different."

The story about Langbo whipping out the book from his pocket during a meeting with the company's environmental people to see if they were on the right track is corny but true. His comment to his people after referring to the book was "Is this what we're really doing?"

"I carry it around in my pocket all the time. I really do," says Langbo.

"That's why we had them printed in two sizes," adds Stewart. "So we could have one in our desk and a pocket-size one to carry around."

Langbo unabashedly adds: "This little book is the glue that holds the company together."

Arthur D. Little

Mission and Guiding Principles

MISSION

We are committed to achieving outstanding value for our clients, rewarding careers for our staff, and excellent performance for our owners.

GUIDING PRINCIPLES

Commitment to Our Clients

We are dedicated to our clients' success and define our own success in terms of theirs. We will strive to understand their needs and to exceed their expectations by delivering practical advice, effective implementation, and innovative product development—always providing outstanding value. And we will continuously renew our resources so that we bring our clients the most up-to-date methodologies and know-how.

Commitment to Our Staff

At Arthur D. Little, the staff members are the firm. We value our own professional well-being and that of our colleagues. We also value our tradition as builders—of outstanding products, services, companies, and businesses. We will provide challenging career paths with ample opportunities for growth and professional development. We will also continue to build our staff capabilities through training, career planning, and effective recruitment. We will uphold our tradition of nurturing creativity, innovation, and teamwork. And we will honor excellence and reward contribution on the part of both individuals and groups.

Commitment to Our Owners

As the owners of Arthur D. Little, we are each personally committed to our company's continuing prosperity and growth. We will strive to enhance the value of the company both by operating profitably and growing our chosen areas and by expanding into promising new ones. We will continue to work together in close cooperation as one company in spirit and purpose worldwide.

Commitment to Quality

We believe that we can best serve our clients, our staff, and our owners by always improving the quality of everything we do. We are committed to the process of becoming a continuously self-improving organization.

Commitment to Integrity

We will make no ethical compromise in pursuit of these goals.

If the client succeeds, so do they.

The Arthur D. Little company was more than a hundred years old before they decided that they needed a mission statement.

"In 1990 we were growing our activities and wanted to make sure that we were clear about where we were and where we wanted to head as an international management, technology, and consulting company," says Alfred E. Wechsler, senior vice president and chief professional officer. His responsibility includes implementation of the company's policies and programs related to development, quality assurance, and management of client assignments, and this includes the mission statement.

"We were changing our overall business strategy, redefining what our core businesses were. We said, 'Wouldn't it be nice if we could put together something that reflects where we are and where we're going.' We already had some policies and documents that reflected our business behavior, but they weren't called *Mission and Guiding Principles* and they weren't in one place," says Wechsler.

The Cambridge, Massachusetts-based firm was founded in 1886 near Harvard and MIT. More than just another business consultancy, Arthur D. Little also invents and develops products (over 3,000 patents have been issued to Little researchers; the company also exploits inventions through Arthur D. Little Enterprises) and owns one of the largest polling companies in the U.S. (Opinion Research Corporation). They also have the distinction of being the only private company that has its own business school. Arthur D. Little Management Education Institute is an accredited school that offers a Master of Science in Management degree.

In writing their own mission statement, Arthur D. Little took a simple tack. "The process for writing was a top-down approach based on some work done by our corporate management group—senior vice presidents in marketing, human resources, finances, and operating management. We had looked at mission statements from other companies, and we put ours together through interviews with staff members and others." Wechsler adds: "When it was written, we tried it out on a broad range of staff to see if they had any comments, and then we sent it out to everyone."

The *Mission and Guiding Principles* is given to all new employees and used in training. "It's also posted in conference rooms and offices worldwide, and we think we do a good job of sharing it with our employees and customers," says Wechsler. "We put it in conference rooms so our customers can see it. We want them to know what our commitment to them is." **We are committed to achieving outstanding value to our clients . . . We are dedicated to our clients' success and define our own success in terms of theirs.**

Wechsler says that the commitment to owners is an important aspect of the mission statement. "Our staff are, in fact, the owners, so shareholder values are important to all our owners." **At Arthur D. Little, the staff members are the firm.**

The mission statement makes reference to the company **becoming a continuously self-improving organization.** "At the time we were preparing the *Mission and Guiding Principles* we were implementing total quality management in the company," Wechsler says. "One thing we ended up doing was including it in the mission statement. It's part of a business concept we call the *high performance organization or business* and it holds that we must satisfy the key stakeholders—customers, employees, and owners. We satisfy them through processes that are being carried out. We continually try to define business processes in our own organization and try to improve these processes. We look at all internal and external processes and try to improve them."

This also means that the company will strive to improve the *Mission and Guiding Principles.* "I think that if we're committed to becoming a self-improving organization, then we are obligated to, on a reasonably regular basis, make sure that our *Mission and Guiding Principles* are indeed the ones that we want to strive to achieve," says Wechsler. "We do look at them and think about updating them, but it's been only a few years since it was prepared, and we're not changing our mission in any particular way. I don't see it changing in any way soon."

The section on integrity, which comes last, is one of the most succinct seen in mission statements. **We will make no ethical compro-**

mise in pursuit of these goals. While it's no surprise that Arthur D. Little has made a commitment to integrity—many companies do—it's a trait that is especially crucial to the consultant business. "In the consulting business that really is a key success factor. Once you have any dealings that show poor business ethics then you might as well close the door and send the employees home," says Wechsler.

Lowe's

Lowe's Vision

Lowe's is in the business of providing the products to help our customers build, improve and enjoy their homes. Our goal is to outservice the competition and be our customers' 1st Choice Store for these products.

The new focus is retail and female.

Power ties are out, power tools are in; Gucci is out, gardening is in; forget TV's "Dallas," think "Home Improvement." That's what the management at the Lowe's Companies says, and it has become the unofficial slogan of the hardware company. The official slogan is the *Vision*, which was developed in 1990 to coincide with the retooling of the company and changes in America's culture.

Lowe's first *Vision* was published on February 1, 1990. "That date, February 1, 1990, has become significant for us," says Cliff Oxford, senior vice president for corporate relations. "Before then, the contractor customer truly was king. On that day, it changed. We had a grouping of 250 stores in 1990, and even though we had been working to develop our retail business, we still had a corporate culture where the store manager was focusing a great deal of attention on building and growing contractor sales. We had been served well with contractor sales for decades, but it was our desire to be a growth company. Leonard [Herring, president and chief executive officer] and his staff knew they had to go about the task of convincing our people in 250 stores that this was the way to go—that we had to leave our old method of operation and develop a mindset for people to realize that their future growth and prosperity was dealing with that retail customer."

This vehicle for massive change was their *Vision*.

. . . **Providing the products to help our customers build, improve and enjoy their homes.** This is the major tenet of the refocusing effort of the company. Herring explains: "This *Vision* says we are only going to sell products that relate to the home. An item has to fit within this statement in order for us to carry it in the stores."

The 1980s were a decade of change for Lowe's. "We were originally a contractor sales company, selling building materials to both new home builders and major subcontractors. That was roughly seventy percent of our business; the other thirty percent was directly to the public. Most of the dollar volume was to the professional trade," Herring says.

Then the housing crunch hit, and Lowe's sales and earnings were affected by the downturn in building. If Lowe's was to continue their earlier pattern of growth, something drastic had to be done. "We realized that the retail portion of our business was more stable than the contractor portion," says Herring. "Although we had no intention of giving up our contractor sales volume, we thought that if we could build our retail business to a larger percentage of the total, we could have a more stable business and then take advantage of the housing industry when it became available again."

One of the first things they did to attract more retail customers was to establish a Lowe's credit card. The next step was improvements to the stores themselves. "At that time, our sales floor in our stores was roughly ten thousand square feet," says Herring. "We went into these sales floors and did a considerable amount of work on the signage, lighting, and pricing—things that would make the store more attractive to the retail customer."

Lowe's, by having been so strongly associated with the contractor business, had completely missed a huge group of potential customers —women. The company decided to focus much of its attention to this group. Says Herring: "One of our primary interests was to develop a store and develop a product line that would entice more females to shop at our stores. We knew they spent a lot of money. The products that we wanted to sell, such as home decor, paint, locksets, and moldings, were all selected by the woman in the home. We wanted her to visit our stores. We slanted our advertising and our product that way."

And slowly, during the 1980s, Lowe's brightened their stores, remodeled them, and increased their sales floor square footage. By 1987 they were only building supply "superstores" with 45,000 and 65,000 square feet. "We realized that we could operate larger stores successfully and make a good return on our investment," Herring says.

. . . to outservice the competition and be our customers' 1st Choice . . . "Lowe's is not an item merchant, we are a project merchant," says Oxford. "K marts and Wal-Marts are item merchants. We want you to come in and buy related items to build a deck. In order to accomplish that, we have to have the best-trained personnel to give you a level of confidence that they know what they're talking about when they tell you how to build a deck, hang wallpaper, or hang a light fixture. It's also having more services available to retailers, such as cutting boards, cutting glass, designing kitchens, and delivering and installing products."

He adds: "The female consumer is extremely important to Lowe's. That's where the new growth had been stemming from, and yet here you had a store manager who was accustomed to dealing with [male] builders and contractors. Think of a scenario where there's a contractor waiting in line and you know he has a two-thousand-dollar order, and there's a young mother in line with her child asking about sixty-nine-cent lightbulbs. The *Vision* has truly refocused managers' attention on a totally new business that was previously our minority business. We realized in 1989 that we had to have this idea in writing so that everyone was playing from the same piece of music."

Lowe's *Vision* consists of only two sentences. "This vision really started off being a two-page document," says Oxford. "It took many weeks to refine and revise down to its present state." Herring put together a think tank including himself, Lowe's merchandising manager, and the store operations manager, along with an outside consultant. "It went through many revisions and meetings over a ninety-day period," confirms Herring. "It was done very slowly and with some difficulty."

Lowe's employees had a financial stake in adapting the new corporate philosophy. If it was successful, they all stood to make a lot of money. Lowe's has an employee stock option program (ESOP) available to full-time employees after a thousand hours of work, and the employees own 25 percent of the company. Therefore, following the new corporate direction became crucial for each employee personally.

This new focus has been very successful for Lowe's. "About a decade ago the split between contractor and retail sales was fifty-fifty," says Oxford. "Today eighty percent of sales is to the retail consumer. Twenty percent is contractor, and that's without losing any contractor dollars."

"We have stuck to our *Vision*, and it has allowed us to take a very complex business and try to simplify it so we're all working toward the same goal," says Oxford. "It has positioned this company to grow substantially during the balance of this decade."

Marriott

Mission

Grow a worldwide lodging business using Total Quality Management (TQM) principles to continuously improve preference and profitability. *Our commitment is that <u>every guest leaves satisfied.</u>*

Vision

We will shape our future as a global organization that grows and prospers by:

1. Being completely focused on satisfying each of our customers, earning their trust and loyalty, and creating long-term relationships with them.

2. Always embodying the ideals of the Marriott Philosophy, most importantly the belief that taking care of associates is the key to long-term success. We will:
   - Treat people fairly, ethically, honestly, and in a caring manner.
   - Offer each of our diverse associates the opportunity and training to grow to their full potential professionally while maintaining a balance between work and personal needs.
   - Remove any barriers to promoting women and minorities into all levels of management.
   - Create an environment where all are empowered to care for customers and associates; an environment that is both enjoyable and productive, where each role or job is meaningful and important, where team work is the norm and pride is evident.

3. Using Total Quality Management to pioneer new levels of customer satisfaction and value, becoming a model for organizations around the world. We will:

   - Seek continuous improvement by encouraging initiative, candor, constructive conflict, innovation, and risk-taking.
   - Support those who surface problems to solve and ways to improve our performance.

4. Building profitable, long-term relationships with our extended family of distributors, franchisees, lenders, owners, shareholders, suppliers, and the communities in which we work.

"Every guest leaves satisfied."

Marriott's current *Mission* and *Vision* were written in the early 1990s. William R. Tiefel, executive vice president of Marriott International and president of the Marriott Lodging Group, describes the process: "Like many companies, we had trouble with terminology. What's a mission statement, what's a vision? Basically we started with a vision statement, which we saw as something lofty, not what we were, but what we wanted to be.

Marriott's *Vision* starts out with focusing on customer satisfaction. How do you determine customer satisfaction in the hotel business? "We have some very good tracking systems," says Tiefel. "We have about eight hundred thousand responses in our guest service summaries. We're trying to have customers tell us what we do right and wrong, and they do a very good job of it. We have five million members of Marriott's Honor Guest Award Program. We have a methodology within that group where they can give award recognition in their own name to our employees. It's signed by me, so they've become known as Tiefel awards." These methodologies seem to be working for Marriott. "We think we are getting good information and have put problem resolution as the major game-plan initiative for 1994, along with consistency and training."

The second point of the *Vision* deals with their associates. The **balance between work and personal needs** is something that many companies don't think of putting in a vision statement. But Marriott feels different. "We're working hard on this," says Tiefel. "We have a very strong work ethic that starts with the Marriott family and a competitiveness that makes people want to work really hard. We have to chase people away from work. Senior management leadership is very important here. One of the ways to accomplish this is to not be an absolute drone yourself. Don't stay late, don't work weekends. This is not a marathon. We're not trying to outwork each other." One way Marriott tries to achieve a balance in these areas is through their work/family department. "It's a key department here, involving activities such as day care, and financial advice for lower-compensated employees," says Tiefel.

Create . . . an environment that is both enjoyable and productive . . . This is tough for any company. Marriott stepped away from its traditional, conservative stance and tried something new—casual day. "The cheapest benefit we ever put in was casual day. We've always been a shirt-and-tie place. We fretted over this. We didn't like the idea, but we tried it during the summer one Friday a month; then we did it year-round once a month; now we do it every Friday," says Tiefel. "I believe the morale on Friday is higher than any other day. It's a small step forward, but a big morale booster."

Using Total Quality Management to pioneer new levels of customer satisfaction and value, becoming a model for organizations around the world is the third point of the Marriott *Vision*. "TQM is customer focus," says Tiefel. "It's benchmarking the right issues, the right people, the right competitors. It's the business of constant improvement. For me, it helps people to embrace change. We're having some fair success in changing, but people have to stop being afraid of change," he says.

The *Vision* has not changed substantially since it was first written in 1991. "The *Vision* is a guiding light for us about where we want to go in the future, what we want to be," says Tiefel. "Given our success in accomplishing this, we will be writing another vision statement in the future. We haven't achieved all the goals in this vision, but we're working on it," he says.

The Marriott *Mission* statement was developed along with the original *Vision* statement, but it is more grounded in the present. "The *Mission* statement gets down to where we want to be positioned in the world of business," says Tiefel.

Grow[ing] a worldwide lodging business . . . is crucial to Marriott's success. "We have been rather parochial," says Tiefel. "We're largely a U.S. company. I'm preaching that we've got to be global to be competitive. The opportunities for us are enormous. So we wanted to use the word 'worldwide.' The more our people embrace that, the more they're comfortable with it when we announce that we're opening in Buenos Aires, or that we're now in Singapore. In fact, we're now in twenty countries with forty hotels overseas and many more to come. We've got plans to double our system distribution in the next five to eight years. Worldwide is important," he says.

. . . **continuously improve preference and profitability** is of great concern to Tiefel. "You've got to have both in balance to be successful in this business," he says.

The last sentence of the *Mission* statement was not in the original version. This sentence was added after a management meeting in March 1993. ***Our commitment is that every guest leaves satisfied.*** "This is our rallying cry, our call to arms," says Tiefel. "The management liked the *Mission* statement, but our housekeepers, our bell staff, our waiters and waitresses, our cooks, said, 'Where do I stand in all this worldwide lodging business?' " Tiefel replied: "Where you come in is that if the guest leaves satisfied, you have contributed to and embraced the *Mission* statement."

Marriott did something a little differently when writing their *Vision* and *Mission* statements. The executive committee of Marriott Hotels went on a retreat to work out their vision and mission. Each of the twenty-two executives was asked to write his or her own, individual mission statements. Tiefel explains: "All twenty-two of us each got up and read ours to the group. A smaller group of our better writers took them all and synthesized them into one document. Then, in September of 1991, we brought together all of the general managers and senior staff—about 450 people—at our headquarters in Washington. I read the *Vision* statement. We gave everyone a chance to read it, make some comments that day, and then over the next two weeks discuss it with their people and give us feedback. So everybody in each hotel was working on this statement. They were also told to come up with a vision statement for their own hotel. Some took lines from the corporate vision. Some said, 'This is just fine for us.' "

Tiefel summed up Marriott's commitment to customer satisfaction, the main focus of their *Vision* and *Mission* statements, by saying: "Now we're working on how to *delight* customers."

DECLARATION OF STRATEGIC INTENT

MERCK & CO., INC.

Princeton, New Jersey, U.S.A.   **May 1993**

OUR MISSION

The mission of Merck & Co., Inc., is to provide society with superior products and services — innovations and solutions that satisfy customer needs and improve the quality of life — to provide employees with meaningful work and advancement opportunities and investors with a superior rate of return.

OUR CORE VALUES

1. We value above all our ability to serve all who can benefit from the appropriate use of our products and services, thereby providing lasting consumer and customer satisfaction. We are in the business of preserving and improving human life. All of our actions must be measured by our success in achieving this goal.

2. We are commited to the highest standards of ethics and integrity. We are responsible to our customers, to our employees, to the environments we inhabit and to the societies we serve around the world. In discharging our responsibilities, we do not take professional or ethical shortcuts. Our interactions with our environments and with all segments of society — our customers, our suppliers, governments and the general public — must reflect the high standards we profess.

3. We are dedicated to achieving the highest level of scientific excellence and commit our research to maintaining human health and improving the quality of life. We continually strive to identify the most critical needs of consumers and customers and devote our resources to meeting those needs.

4. We expect profit, but profit from work that satisfies customer needs and that benefits humanity. Our ability to discharge our responsibilities depends on maintaining a financial position that invites investment in leading-edge research and which makes possible effective delivery of research results.

5. We recognize that the ability to most competitively meet consumer and customer needs depends on the knowledge, imagination, skills, teamwork and integrity of our employees, and we value these qualities most highly.

OUR FUTURE

Merck & Co., Inc., is being confronted with wave upon wave of dramatic changes. We must rise to the challenge of these changes and accept that different eras demand different managerial values, skills, behaviors and competencies. Regardless of how success is measured, we will be only as successful as our customers allow us to be. Successfully meeting customer needs demands a management behavior that values speed, flexibility, agility and simplicity. To assimilate these management values into our culture we must:

Communicate

Create and communicate a sense of vision and shared values. Keep employees personally informed about the progress toward, and their role in, achieving operating and strategic objectives.

Develop

Seek the very best talent, without compromise, and ensure the appropriate skills to achieve operating and strategic objectives through life-long learning.

Empower

Create conditions that enable achieving operating and strategic objectives. Encourage initiative and prudent risk taking and refrain from penalizing related failures. Accept responsibility for failures as well as for successes. Engage in team building and remove unproductive organizational barriers.

Lead

Strike a balance between the openness and flexibility that encourages creativity and the follow-up and decisiveness needed to achieve operating and strategic objectives. Eliminate all unnecessary work and encourage quantum-leap improvements. Change before we have to in order to control our own destiny. Optimize the benefits of a diverse work force.

Reward

Provide candid, fair and honest performance evaluations. Provide financial and other compensation mechanisms that encourage and recognize team excellence as well as individual accomplishment.

Guidance for an Uncertain Future in Health Care

Merck & Company, Inc., was named the most admired company in America by *Forbes* magazine for seven years in a row.

Their mission statement is one sentence long and part of a document called the *Declaration of Strategic Intent*. This document also includes a section called *Our Core Values* and a section on *Our Future*. According to J. Douglas Phillips, executive director, strategic planning and analysis, the *Declaration* was created to meet three needs: (1) To place greater emphasis on being consumer- and customer-focused; (2) To expand their innovative solutions to include services as well as products; and (3) To foster organizational speed, flexibility, simplicity, and agility in meeting consumer and customer needs.

"A mission statement should be somewhat evergreen, but specific enough to give you guidance," says Phillips. "What we did last year is we exploded this out a little to begin to lay the groundwork to broaden our horizon. Our vision is to go beyond just innovative products," he says.

The unique part of the document, and one of the reasons it's called a *Declaration* is that it was signed by all of the 450 senior managers in a May 1993 meeting where it was unveiled. Says Robin Hogen, executive director of corporate public affairs and president of the Merck Foundation, "We had a senior management meeting to discuss trends and current environment, future environment for the company, and to, in effect, embrace a new vision for Merck, which was later played out in our acquisition of Medco Containment Services."

Following the unveiling of their new mission statement in May 1993, Merck announced the acquisition of Medco Containment Services. "The mission statement came first, but we were working on the Medco deal all along," says Hogen. "We're the first pharmaceutical company to be vertically integrated. One of the frustrations of being in the pharmaceutical business is that you have to sell to doctors and then they decide whether to prescribe your medicine. We're removed from interaction with the patient. With Medco, we have interaction with thirty-eight million customers. [Medco is the largest pharmaceutical benefits management company in the U.S.] Medco carries all lines of medicines, but we are always the preferred product," he says.

"Everyone knew that this would be a short-term mission statement," says Phillips. "We are in a tremendous period of change and volatility. **Merck & Co., Inc., is being confronted with wave upon wave of dramatic changes.** We're fine-tuning our thoughts, and our first step was in coordinated pharmaceutical care. Our next step, if we're going to be a player in the health care system, is to go beyond pharmaceutical. Conceptually, if you think about where health care is going, the focus has changed. We're moving from a focus on illness to a focus on wellness; we're moving from episodic care to planned care; we're moving from being treatment oriented to outcome oriented; we're moving from cost shifting to cost sharing; and we're moving from profits being made from utilizations to profits being made from non-utilizations. The way it's going to work is you're going to make your money from people staying away from the doctor's office, away from the hospital, and away from drugs. How will Merck participate in that? We've got to get beyond just being a pharmaceutical manufacturer. We've got to get into health care management in a broader base," he says.

"Now the mission statement talks about **superior products and services,** and now we also talk about innovative solutions which are not necessarily products," says Phillips. "If you look at Dr. Vagelos's [chairman and CEO] speech to the shareholders, he alludes to the next step of the mission statement. What we're really talking about is integrated health systems. To get beyond just the manufacturing and delivering of a pharmaceutical product to the end user. We started to expand our horizons in this mission statement to innovative solutions and services without tipping our hand about things like the Medco acquisition. But it's going to go beyond that. The next generation of the mission statement will not take place until we get a new CEO. (Dr. Vagelos was expected to retire in November 1994.) We are working on a recommended mission statement for the new CEO to approve. This statement will recognize that we are going to broaden our horizons toward integrated health care systems."

The values section of their *Declaration* really speaks to the reasons that Merck has enjoyed such a stellar reputation. "Our employees feel good working for a company that's saving lives," says Hogen. "Whether it's by vaccinating children or potentially curing prostate cancer, the bottom line is a better life for millions of people. The idea of providing **society with superior products and services** that improve the quality of life is something held very dear at Merck. We've been as bold to say in some of our literature and orientation films that Merck has probably saved more lives and extended the lives of more people than any other company in the world. There's no way for us to qualify that; there's no data to support that. But we are the largest pharmaceutical company in the world with the largest product line. We deal with prime disease. We don't make Band-Aids and cough syrups. We make drugs that keep people alive. When people feel that, it does build great loyalty and pride in the enterprise," Hogen concludes.

Motorola

TOTAL CUSTOMER SATISFACTION

KEY BELIEFS—*how we will always act*
- Constant Respect for People
- Uncompromising Integrity

KEY GOALS—*what we must accomplish*
- Best in Class
  - *—People*
  - *—Marketing*
  - *—Technology*
  - *—Product: Software, Hardware and Systems*
  - *—Manufacturing*
  - *—Service*
- Increased Global Market Share
- Superior Financial Results

KEY INITIATIVES—*how we will do it*
- Six Sigma Quality
- Total Cycle Time Reduction
- Product, Manufacturing and Environmental Leadership
- Profit Improvement
- Empowerment for all, in a Participative, Cooperative and Creative Workplace

Only 3.4 errors per million?

M otorola's mission statement seems to explain the obvious on one side of a card:

OUR FUNDAMENTAL OBJECTIVE
(Everyone's Overriding Responsibility)
Total Customer Satisfaction

"A corporation is an orchestra," says Bob Galvin, son of the company's founder Paul Galvin and chairman of the executive committee. "Many elements, constantly trying to blend harmonies. At any given point in time one part may or may not be in harmony. It may be too loud, for instance. In our corporation, each of us can think the center of the universe is our department. In the mission statement we thought it was valuable to emphasize the obvious—that this is a very personal responsibility. The word *everyone* is quite significant, because it means not one of us is left out. It means that I am exclusively and directly responsible, but so are the rest of you. We are a team."

Motorola is widely known for its team approach in all areas. The company is on a continuing program to decentralize units which sometimes leads to turf wars and tension among and between different units and teams. Although the card itself doesn't dissolve tensions, its contribution in building esprit de corps and keeping everyone focused on the ultimate goals of the company does help mitigate turf battles and animosity among the different units and teams, according to Galvin.

On the customer-satisfaction phrase, Galvin says: "We ask employees to use their common sense when it comes to customer satisfaction. There is no definition you can memorize about what customer satisfaction is all about. You have to go out to the customer and find that out for yourself. You make sure that the customer doesn't have anything to complain or worry about. You know darn well if you've served your customers," says Galvin. "You know perfectly well what else that customer expected. If not, then you better go learn it."

The other side of the card contains sections on **Key Beliefs**—*how we will always act;* **Key Goals**—*what we must accomplish;* and **Key Initiatives**—*how we will do it.*

Despite Motorola's hard-driving reputation, its main focus is people, as in **Constant Respect for People.** "I know this sounds corny and old-fashioned, but my father got us off on the right foot from the start. The largest portion of the mix of Motorola employees were women. They put radios together. (Galvin's father established the first factory for commercially produced car radios in 1929. The name Motorola was a combination of the words *motor* and *Victrola*.) I know how he felt about his mother and my guess is that my father subliminally saw his mother as he looked down at the production line. Wouldn't you treat your mom with first-class respect? It's just about that simple. We [Motorola] discovered that there wasn't any better self-interest in the world than to treat the other person with respect. It's been a pretty simple culture. We stumble every once in while, thoughtlessness or something else, but there's no intention."

Motorola is nonunion, has about 120,000 employees, and still maintains a family atmosphere. Son Christopher Galvin is now company president.

One of the **Key Goals** is to be **Best in Class,** and Galvin believes this is true for people as well as for corporations. Indeed, that's why people are mentioned first again. "From a competitive standard we can't be as good as our competition unless you're as good as your counterpart at the other company. It's clear that Mr. Kobiashi [former chairman of NEC, who had the vision to realize that communications and computers were intertwined and so set his company on that course] is smarter than I am, so I'd better go learn some more. It puts me on a track aspiring to be way better than I am. I never knew if I had caught up to Mr. Kobiashi or not, but at least all the time he was around I was striving to be as good as he," says Galvin.

Under **Key Initiatives,** the mission statement talks about **Six Sigma Quality.** This factor alone may be responsible for Motorola's success.

Sigma is the eighteenth letter of the Greek alphabet, and to business statisticians it signifies a measurement of defects. Motorola's mission statement calls for the lofty goal of Six Sigma Quality, which translates to 3.4 mistakes per million. Six Sigma applies to the thousands of individual processes and elements involved in producing, say, a cellular phone. "We have reached Six Sigma in lots of places," says Galvin, "about twenty to twenty-five percent of our measurable activities—a small department here, a large department somewhere else. On average we're about 5.55. Nothing can happen [i.e., no product is sold or process considered worthy] until we're at five. If they [processes or parts] were to degrade [above five] we would shut them down."

The mission statement also calls for **Total Cycle Time Reduction.** "In that area, we're doing rather well," Galvin says. "Quality and cycle time reduction are reciprocals of each other. If one improves one's quality, you have shorter steps, less time in between steps, less preparing. You get from beginning to end in less time." By reducing defects and cycle time, Motorola estimates it saved $1.5 billion in 1993. Company officials hope to decrease its error rate ten times every year and cut its cycle time ten times every five years.

These cuts in error rates and production time are particularly crucial to the company's integrated chip operations, where it is the world's third-largest manufacturer behind Intel and NEC. Motorola, IBM, and Apple joined together to produce the PowerPC chip for personal computers in an effort to unseat Intel's dominant slot.

Galvin says he won't take credit for Motorola's mission statement. "I am just the media. I put it on the card, and the idea for putting it on the card came from the Ford Motor Company. It's a class of media that is easy to digest. It contains significant information."

Galvin, former chairman and CEO, is being modest. What he doesn't tell you unless you ask is that he was the driving force behind the electronics and communications company's highly admired and successful total quality management program begun about ten years ago, when the mission-statement-on-a-card was first introduced. The program, which is the subject of countless business school reports and case studies, is responsible for Motorola winning the Baldrige Award and being the only American company whose cellular phones and pagers are of a high enough quality level to be permitted to be sold in Japan.

In 1993, Motorola's worldwide sales reached a record $17 billion. Earnings were $1 billion. Not only are they the sole American manufacturer of pagers, they control 85 percent of the world market.

Galvin says that the card is used by employees in many different ways, much of it in fun. "We really expect that all of us are carrying this card with us. We create circumstances in informal and lighthearted ways of pulling the card and doing something clever with it. It's a signification that we're still attentive to the issues, and that we become denuded by not having it with us. When we find somebody who doesn't have the card, we admonish them in a lighthearted way. The card's substance is the most significant thing, but the card itself, from the point of view of getting along with people, has all manner of utility."

THE NORTHWESTERN MUTUAL WAY

HE ambition of The Northwestern has been less to be large than to be safe ; its aim is to rank first in benefits to policyowners rather than first in size. Valuing quality above quantity, it has preferred to secure its business under certain salutary restrictions and limitations rather than to write a much larger business at the possible sacrifice of those valuable points which have made The Northwestern pre-eminently the policyowner's Company ❖ ❖ ❖ ❖ ❖

Executive Committee · 1888

Providing guidance for 107 years.

The first phrase in *The Northwestern Mutual Way* is contradictory to most big business thinking: **The ambition of The Northwestern has been less to be large than to be safe . . .** "We are a financial institution, so we do have a duty to be safe," says James D. Ericson, president and chief executive officer. "This means we are relatively conservative, but not risk-averse. We do take risks, but we balance risk, which gives us greater safety. If we're going to take risk, we're going to get paid for it. We'll get a higher interest rate or higher return in general," he says. Safety applies not only to the investments they make on behalf of their policyholders but also to accepting someone into the Northwestern insurance family as a policyholder. "We will sell rated policies for people who have certain medical problems, but we charge for it," says Ericson.

Paying claims is a big part of making the company's reputation what it is today. "We go out of our way to pay claims and not deny them," says Ericson. Two stories Ericson relates support that. The first one is about a couple who wanted to insure their newborn. The doctor had not sent the medical records and they had written and called repeatedly to get the forms. Finally, their agent called the parents to solicit their help, and the parents told the agent that their baby had died of sudden infant death syndrome (SIDS) the night before. The agent called the home office and said that if the doctor had gotten the forms to the company promptly, they would have underwritten the baby, and if they had qualified, the company would have written the policy. So she called the doctor again and this time he sent the records. Northwestern found that they would have underwritten the child, so they issued a policy on the deceased child and paid the claim.

Another story repeated throughout the company concerned a married man in his thirties with a family. He had not paid the quarterly premium on his life insurance policy and disregarded the reminders sent by the company, causing the policy to lapse. Six months later, the wife called Northwestern, thinking that they still had a policy. She was calling to let them know that her husband had been diagnosed with a brain tumor and had only a short time to live. She was told the policy had lapsed and normally that is all the action any other insurance company would have taken. But the agent later remembered the wife saying to him that the husband had been making illogical decisions for the past few months, perhaps due to his tumor. The agent called the head office and the company decided to investigate. Northwestern decided that the husband had been impaired by the tumor prior to the lapse of the policy and the policy was reinstated.

Why did they do this? Because their credo directed them to do it, Ericson says. "The key to this is not only our claims policy, but that our agents get very close to people. The mission statement guides the sales force and gives them purpose. It makes them needs-sellers, people looking to solve problems instead of just making a sale. Every speech I give to the sales force is peppered with the credo. This past spring, the 1888 statement was the major topic of my speeches to the sales force."

The phrase **salutary restrictions** originated in the nineteenth century. "There are certain restrictions on how we sell policies," says Ericson. "Today it would be called 'suitability.' The credos we have carved in granite around here have the original wording. The statements we have hung around the office update the phrase."

"The big things in the statement are the idea of safety or trusteeship and the idea of quality over quantity," says Ericson. "Tied all together is the idea that this is the policy holders' company and we run the company for the benefit of the policyholders. That's really where the strength and power of a mutual company comes to bear. As a mutual company, the people who are the policyholders are also the owners. We treat them as both. We're one of the few companies that value their owners more than their customers. With us, you're a customer once, but you're an owner for probably thirty or forty years. We're very careful that we always treat old policyholders fairly. We are in a long-term business," he says.

Northwestern Mutual Life is the tenth largest insurance company in the country and the fiftieth largest U.S. company in terms of assets. It has never received less than the top financial rating from the four major rating services.

"The credo has served us well," says Ericson. For the hundredth anniversary of the mission statement they appointed a special committee of the board to see if they could update it. "After a lot of work, we found no reason to," says Ericson. "We found it to be more modern now than it was then. It really puts forth what this company stands for, and I believe it's what we live by. It does guide what we do."

Northwestern's credo is literally chiseled in stone in their new building in Milwaukee. Every conference room has it too. Ericson's office has a three-by-four-foot replica of it. "We think most of our success flows from everyone understanding this statement," says Ericson. "All decisions are based on the credo, from my office to the clerical offices. Employees embrace this with a great deal of pride," he says.

Ericson sums up by saying: "The mission statement for us is a wonderful tradition and it really does guide the company. It provides marvelous glue that holds everything together and really gives us purpose."

The Park Lane Group

Our Mission

The Park Lane Group is a leader in building, developing, and managing radio stations in small and medium-sized markets. Park Lane and our member stations provide extraordinary service to the communities in which we operate, outstanding growth and development opportunities for our people, and significant returns to our investors. Stations of The Park Lane Group are role models which set a standard for quality small-medium market radio, and The Park Lane Group is a model of outstanding radio group development and management.

OUR PRINCIPLES

The Park Lane Group believes in the importance of . . .

- *Winning through Excellence*—Doing what's right, doing what we do as well as we can do it, and winning as a result of our commitment to excellence.
- *Leadership*—In all aspects of broadcasting, management, and community service, we are out in front, blazing trails, showing the way.
- *Innovation*—We share a need to dream, create, experiment, be adventuresome, because not to change is a sure ticket to becoming old and tired—and defeated.
- *Personal and Professional Development*—For all involved with The Park Lane Group: our listeners, our suppliers, our clients, our communities, and ourselves. We are committed to ensuring personal and professional growth and achievement for all. When one wins, all win.
- *Community Service*—The Park Lane Group and its people are involved, active, aware, and concerned contributors to our communities.
- *Growth*—Because not to grow is to fall behind. We have a mission to

fulfill and a sense of urgency to drive forward every day toward the achievement of our goals.

OUR STATIONS

- Are responsible to uphold the public trust conveyed by our licenses to broadcast and to serve our communities.
- Are programmed to entertain, inform, and serve the needs of our listeners, clients, and communities.
- Are creative, innovative, and fun in programming, marketing, and promotion.
- Are in business to serve our clients and help them grow and prosper with us.
- Are fair and equitable in everything we do. The Park Lane Group and its people operate at all times with the utmost honesty and integrity.

OUR PEOPLE

- Have Vision—We are looking ahead at all times, setting goals for ourselves, our stations, and the Group, and contributing to the achievement of those goals.
- Are Responsible—To themselves, their fellow Group members, and our listeners, clients, suppliers, and communities. We are here to serve dependably and deliver on our promises.
- Are Honest, Fair, and Reliable—We always operate with the utmost integrity.
- Communicate Freely and Openly—We believe in the ability of everyone to contribute to the development and growth of The Park Lane Group and feel free to communicate our thoughts and ideas to others in the Group, while acting responsibly to protect the best interests of Park Lane and all of its people.
- Have a Sense of Urgency—We believe in our mission and understand that there is no time like now to do what we need to do to achieve our goals and fulfill our mission.

The whole must be greater than the sum of its parts.

Jim Levy is passionate about mission statements. "A mission statement must be written as if you are accomplishing it, not as if you're going to. What we're saying to our people is that you have to measure everything you do against this."

Levy wrote the *Our Mission* and *Our Principles* for his broadcasting company, The Park Lane Group, which he formed in 1990. Park Lane now owns and operates eleven radio stations in Arizona and California. Levy is chairman and chief executive officer as well as co-owner with his wife, Marcia Klein Levy.

Each station in The Park Lane Group has its own mission statement as well, and it is revisited annually. When Park Lane acquires a broadcast property, one of the first things they do is write a mission statement. "First we spend about two days tearing apart current reality," says Levy. "We tear apart the station, the competitors, the economic and demographic environment of the community. We review all the issues and the context within which the station operates. Without doing that you can't write a mission statement. You have to define the landscape first. Then you decide, Who do we want to be?—and that's when you write the mission. Sometimes after spending seven or eight hours tearing the issues apart, the mission statement is right there in your face and only takes about fifteen minutes to write. When we define the purpose of a mission statement, I always ask the question 'Why are you here?' The answer is not to make money; that's a by-product.

"When you start to look at who you hire and how you're operating and what you do, the question is 'Does it match that statement?'" Referring to his company's mission statement, he says, "Are you **a leader in building, developing, and managing radio stations**? If it doesn't match, you shouldn't be doing it."

Leadership is a key word for Park Lane. "I tell my people that we have one fundamental objective for leadership. And that is, everyone else says 'That's the way you do it' about us. Everyone wants to work for you. Nobody wants to leave. Everyone in the community looks at you and says you're the leading broadcaster in the community . . . **we are out front, blazing trails, showing the way.** That we set the example for service to the community, for outstanding programming, for great people, for terrific service to clients, for satisfied listeners. If you're going to be the leader, you're going to be the role model.

"Currently in five of our six markets [in many of their markets they own AM and FM stations] we are the leading broadcasters. In the sixth we can't do it with the stand-alone signal we have, so we're in the midst of acquiring a second FM and forming a duopoly. Then, when we put that together, we'll be the leader. That community already sees us as the de facto future leader in the market."

. . . **provide extraordinary service to the communities in which we operate** . . . is a lofty phrase from *Our Mission.* "Here's Levy's four-cornered box of broadcasting," Jim Levy says. "A complete broadcasting operation has to serve four legs of a stool. One leg is community, one leg is listeners, one leg is the clients, and one leg is the employees. All four legs have to be satisfied for you to have a well-rounded operation. I used the word 'extraordinary' because 'extraordinary' implies that you're stepping outside of the norm. You're exceeding the expectations of the community. Ultimately, the only way to provide leadership is to be outside the norm and in front. If your number-one job in the public trust is to serve the community and you want to be the leading broadcaster in a community, then you have to provide extraordinary service, and the word 'extraordinary' is precise."

The last sentence of the mission statement ties the strength of the group into the strength of the stations: . . . **The Park Lane Group is a model of outstanding radio group development and management.** "I wanted to put that in because I think that even if your stations are great, it doesn't mean the group is great. I think they are interconnected in that it takes a great group management to build a complete group of great stations and vice versa. I don't think our stations would be as successful as they are today without the combined strength and talents of the group," says Levy. "And I don't think we would have as much synergy within the group if we hadn't focused on how to make the stations better by utilizing the group. The role of group management is to make sure all the assets of the group are at work at all times and are being used optimally. If you have a problem in one market, you may have the solution in another market.

"When we started Park Lane, it was not with the sense that we would ever sell a station. A lot of groups are investment portfolios. Buy one, build it, and sell it, over and over. So you have a mix of assets. Most of the groups we found in the market size we're involved in were group ownership, but not group management. We felt that a critical part to our success as a group was to have individual stations, but have the group linked up and working together. That is why there is a purposeful statement there as far as group management is concerned, as opposed to just saying we're going to have a group of outstanding radio stations."

In the eleven stations Levy has acquired over the past four years, he hasn't seen a mission statement at any of the stations they've taken over. "Nobody looks beyond tomorrow," he says.

Mission statements seem to be getting the job done for The Park Lane Group, but it's only part of the process, Levy says. "A mission statement is a bull's-eye, not a whole target."

THE
PENNEY
IDEA

To serve the public, as nearly as we can, to its
complete satisfaction.

—————— • — • ——————

To expect for the service we render a fair remuneration
and not all the profit the traffic will bear.

—————— • — • ——————

To do all in our power to pack the customer's dollar full
of value, quality and satisfaction.

—————— • — • ——————

To continue to train ourselves and our associates so that the service
we give will be more and more intelligently performed.

—————— • — • ——————

To improve constantly the human factor in our business.

—————— • — • ——————

To reward men and women in our organization through participation
in what the business produces.

—————— • — • ——————

To test our every policy, method and act in this wise:
"Does it square with what is right and just?"

Adopted 1913

The founder's ideas were way ahead of their time.

In 1913, James Cash Penney and five partners met in a hotel room in Salt Lake City to establish a set of guiding principles to operate and grow the Golden Rule Store Company stores. What came out of that meeting was called the *Original Body of Doctrine*, later changed to *The Penney Idea*. It has stayed virtually the same since then.

To read the seven tenets of *The Penney Idea* you would think they were written in the 1980s or 1990s, and not in 1913, as the concepts embrace management philosophies made popular during the past decade. To understand *The Penney Idea* is to understand Penney himself and what a prescient businessperson he really was.

Penney started as a temporary clerk in a store in Kemmerer, Wyoming, and later was offered a partnership in the small but growing chain known as the Golden Rule stores. "Kemmerer was a typical mining town," says W. R. Howell, current chairman and chief executive officer. "In 1902, people had no real alternative. It was like the old Ernie Ford song: 'I owe my soul to the company store.' Mr. Penney opened up an alternative. It was cash and carry, and he didn't gouge people. He gave them value at a fair price."

This idea of fairness was revolutionary in a time when captive customers in small towns in the West were used to bargaining with retailers about price; it changed constantly based on inventory and demand. A sign proclaiming the "one price" policy was on the outside of the store; Penney and his partners put it down on paper this way: **To expect for the service we render a fair remuneration, and not all the profit the traffic will bear.**

By the end of 1903, the Kemmerer store was rock solid and his partners offered James Cash Penney a one-third interest in the Rock Springs, Wyoming, store if he could increase its sales. He did, and the three opened up another store in Cumberland, Wyoming. Shortly after that venture, his partners offered to sell Penney all three stores. "Reluctantly, he changed the name of the stores to J. C. Penney when he learned that someone in Oregon was also using the name Golden Rule," Howell says.

Penney opened up more stores through partnerships—Penney would own a third share, the manager would own a third, and a sponsoring partner would own a third. Thus followed the Penney idea: **To reward the men and women in our organization through participation in what the business produces.** Giving employees a stake in the company's success was unheard of at the time, but he believed that it motivated people. "Today we at the company think of it as management through partnership," says Howell.

However, Penney was forced to change this way of expanding his stores because bankers didn't feel comfortable lending money to someone with such a nontraditional approach to business. Because of this, Penney incorporated in 1913 and issued stock to the partners in each store. Earnings on shares were distributed based on profits of each store. These days it's done in a more sophisticated way. Howell says, "Now men and women are partners through a profit-sharing program. They are the recipients of our good and bad years. The past year, the match was the highest it has ever been—ninety cents on the dollar."

Penney looked at employees in an innovative way. **To continue to train ourselves and our associates so that the service we give will be more and more intelligently performed.** Note the word *associates*. It's a word that came into vogue in the 1980s to give workers a sense of belonging and empowerment. Penney and his partners used it in 1913. Says Howell: "Subordinate relationships were avoided at all costs." Penney was also a big believer in training. "He accomplished that through personal example. That was his form of training."

But what did he mean by **improve constantly the human factor in our business**? Howell had visited with Penney several times before his death at age ninety-five. This was one of the questions he asked him. "I met with Mr. Penney and this was his explanation: Each generation has higher expectations for the individual person, community, church, and so forth, and his idea was that we must provide a place, the company, for example, where we can better ourselves from one generation to the next because that's what is happening in the world. He talked about improving ourselves as we move forward in our business.

When we try to improve J. C. Penney we sharply focus on the human elements of training, motivation, retention, and so on. They are all important in a labor-intensive business like retailing and cataloging."

Penney associates continue to pledge their support to *The Penney Idea* and the company motto penned in 1913: Honor, Confidence, Service, and Cooperation. This past year the company inducted over a thousand new partners who go through an affirmation ceremony, the same ceremony that Penney associates went through when the company was founded. These inductees have been with the company at least five years and have reached a profit-sharing level of management where a substantial portion of their annual income depends upon the performance of the unit in which they work.

"They take a verbal pledge committing themselves to sustain and protect the partnership. People always say to me: 'I can't believe you can ask people to make a pledge.' Well, I say to them that you ought to try it sometime. I think there's a lot more people who would like to make a commitment to *something* but nobody's asking them to."

During his last remaining years, Penney was filmed speaking about *The Penney Idea* and what it means. These 16-millimeter films were later transferred to videotape and are shown at the induction ceremony. "He is on the screen telling them what he means by honor, confidence, service, and cooperation. We've got Mr. Penney in his own words," says Howell. "The ceremony is just as moving now as when I did it back in the 1970s."

Howell adds: "These seven tenets as put forth in the early teens are timeless. The man was a great visionary and he understood basic fundamental principles. What is so impressive to me is how many of our middle management understand the mission, understand *The Penney Idea* and the commitment to the company."

OUR CORPORATE MISSION

The Reader's Digest Association, Inc. is built on a heritage of service. Today our company is a global publisher and world leader in direct mail marketing. Our magazines, books and home entertainment products provide customers with hours of reading, listening and viewing pleasure. The legacy of service and quality lives on — timeless ideals guiding us in our mission: to profitably develop, produce and market high quality products that enrich, inform and entertain people all over the world.

WORDS WE LIVE BY

Focus on Serving the Customer — Providing superior quality service that meets the individual needs of our customers. Developing and delivering products that make a difference in people's lives worldwide.

Recognition and Concern for Employees — Respecting the individual. Advocating fair treatment for all. Rewarding exceptional performance. Showing commitment to personal and professional growth. Encouraging teamwork.

Maintain High Ethical Standards — Becoming involved as good corporate citizens wherever we work and live around the world. Treating customers and suppliers with integrity, fairness and respect. Avoiding even the appearance of conflict of interest. Respecting and preserving our environment. Providing leadership in industry, trade and regulatory associations.

Innovative, Results-Oriented Company — Dedicating ourselves to maximizing the value of the corporation for share owners.

Yes, of course it has a condensed version.

*R*eader's Digest. We all grew up with them. Our parents read them, and we read them. But in the last decade or so, while the products have remained the same, the way that the company is being run has changed.

Our Corporate Mission, written in 1983, was one of many things used to codify the direction of the company.

Reader's Digest is the flagship of the corporation and was the first product of the company. In 1921 DeWitt and Lila Wallace had a radical idea. Even then, time was a precious commodity and they thought people would buy a magazine full of condensed articles on a host of different topics. "Join an Association of Readers" read Wallace's first circular to drum up subscribers. The Wallaces' idea was a hit, and they published their first monthly issue in February 1922. The Wallaces' *Reader's Digest* was tremendously popular in the twenties and thirties and reached one million subscribers in 1935.

The Wallaces managed the company until the early 1970s. They treated their employees like family, helping them through financial crises, giving Fridays off in the spring, and having very generous vacation policies. After that a succession of long-time employees held the top posts, with DeWitt Wallace still actively involved behind the scenes. In May 1984 veteran Reader's Digest employee George Grune took over as chairman and CEO and he changed the feel of the company, eliminating some of the niceties along with several hundred of the workforce. Instead of the folksy company it once was, it was operating along more traditional corporate lines.

And, like many corporations that had grown out of family operations, they were a bit scattered. One of the phrases coming out of this phase of Reader's Digest's transition was "Get all the arrows going in one direction." The original senior management team were given crystal arrows which adorn their desks even today as reminders of the new focus for the company.

You don't often see a reference to how a company's product is marketed in mission statements, but the Reader's Digest mission statement talks about **direct mail marketing** in the second sentence. Why? Because it is the cornerstone of the business. The Wallaces started the business with their direct mail flyer and it was the reason for their success. In fact, Reader's Digest was the first company to personalize direct mail, and because of this innovation, DeWitt Wallace is in the Direct Marketing Hall of Fame.

The mission statement as it was lasted seven years, until Grune took the company public in 1990. Then it was amended to reflect their new obligation to shareholders. **Dedicating ourselves to maximizing the value of the corporation for share owners.**

Adhering to their ethics as spelled out in *Words We Live By* has cost the company some revenue. For example, neither *Reader's Digest* nor any of their publishing entities accepts any tobacco advertising. This results in millions of lost advertising revenue, but the Wallaces didn't accept it in the beginning and that thought is carried through today. Even acquired magazines have to give up tobacco advertisers.

Copies of the mission statement are framed and hung around the company's headquarters and worldwide offices. It is printed on the back of the employee handbook. It is on the back of the *Global Fact Sheet* sent out to all 6,800 employees. It is in everyone's office, present at all meetings, and often shown by overhead projector to make sure that the outcome of all discussions fits into the corporate mission.

You might have thought all they published was that little book full of condensed articles. But then you would be wrong. Reader's Digest, world-headquartered appropriately enough in Pleasantville, New York, is a global publisher of books, magazines, home videos, and music collections. *Reader's Digest* is their best-known product and is found in every country, territory, and province in the world, the company boasts.

Reader's Digest has 45 editions, is published in 17 languages, and has a circulation of 28 million with a monthly readership of 100 million worldwide. And, as popular as *Reader's Digest* is in the U.S., more than half of its revenue and profit comes from international operations.

While most Reader's Digest employees cannot recite the corporate

Our Corporate Mission verbatim, they can tell you, according to company officials, what else but the condensed version, which is the last line of the mission statement: . . . **to profitably develop, produce and market high quality products that enrich, inform and entertain people all over the world.**

THE RITZ-CARLTON

The Ritz-Carlton® Hotel Company

CREDO

A Ritz-Carlton Hotel
is a place where the genuine care
and comfort of our guests
is our highest mission.

We pledge to provide the finest personal
service and facilities for our guests
who will always enjoy a warm, relaxed
yet refined ambience.

The Ritz-Carlton experience enlivens the
senses, instills well being, and fulfills
even the unexpressed wishes and needs
of our guests.

THE RITZ-CARLTON
HOTEL COMPANY

MISSION STATEMENT

The Ritz-Carlton Hotel Company will be regarded as the quality and market leader
of the hotel industry worldwide.

We are responsible for creating exceptional, profitable results with the investments
entrusted to us by efficiently satisfying customers.

The Ritz-Carlton Hotels will be the clear choice of discriminating business and leisure travelers,
meeting planners, travel industry partners, owners, partners and the travel agent community.

Founded on the principles of providing a high level of genuine, caring, personal service; cleanliness;
beauty; and comfort, we will consistently provide all customers with their ultimate expectation,
a memorable experience and exceptional value. Every employee will be empowered to
provide immediate corrective action should customer problems occur.

Meeting planners will favor The Ritz-Carlton Hotels. Empowered sales staff will know their own product and
will always be familiar with each customer's business. The transition of customer requirements from Sales to
Conference Services will be seamless. Conference Services will be a partner to the meeting planner, with
General Managers showing interest through their presence and participation. Any potential problem will be
solved instantly and with ease for the planner. All billing will be clear, accurate and timely. All of this will create
a memorable, positive experience for the meeting planner and the meeting participants.

Key account customers will receive individualized attention,
products and services in support of their organization's objectives.

All guests and customers will know we fully appreciate their loyalty.

The Ritz-Carlton Hotels will be the first choice for important and social business events
and will be the social centers in each community. Through creativity, detailed planning,
and communication, banquets and conferences will be memorable.

Our restaurants and lounges will be the first choice of
the local community and will be patronized on a regular basis.

The Ritz-Carlton Hotels will be known as positive,
supportive members of their community and will be sensitive to the environment.

The relationships we have with our suppliers will be one of mutual confidence and teamwork.

We will always select employees who share our values. We will strive to meet individual needs because our
success depends on the satisfaction, effort and commitment of each employee. Our leaders will constantly
support and energize all employees to continuously improve productivity and customer satisfaction. This will be
accomplished by creating an environment of genuine care, trust, respect, fairness and teamwork through
training, education, empowerment, participation, recognition, rewards and career opportunities.

To boldly go where no hotel has gone before.

"The Ritz-Carlton Hotel Company's current *Mission Statement* is less than two years old," says Patrick Mene, corporate director of quality. "The original *Mission Statement*, penned in 1983, was modified in July 1993 by the sixteen senior leaders of the company. The Senior Quality Management Team asked the entire company 'for whom are they trying to do what, and how?' " and the *Mission Statement* developed from there, says Mene. "The new *Mission Statement* deals more with the means by which we'll be more competitive and profitable and attractive. It describes the process a little more by which we'll be effective, not just the output in terms of economic performance."

Meeting planners will favor The Ritz-Carlton Hotels. One of the new focuses of the *Mission Statement* is on specific customers such as meeting planners, an area management felt needed improvement. Meeting planners represent a substantial revenue source for the Ritz-Carlton. "Just about half of our business comes from meetings," says Mene. "We thought it would be beneficial to be very explicit about the requirements of the people that fund half of the system," he says. "We have initiated a formal system to listen to planners. Then the quality staff follows up."

Any potential problem will be solved instantly and with ease for the planner. "The meeting planner, who has a lot of customers, is really customizing a specific product with us. Their needs from the direct sales part of the organization are specific needs and then when they go into the pre-event phase there are other specific needs. Then there's the event phase—the hotel stay. Then postevent: there's a lot of special requirements in terms of very complicated billing," says Mene. "It was such an important market segment, we wanted to teach the organization how important they were and tell them their specific needs, so we actually made it a part of our *Mission Statement*."

Key account customers will receive individualized attention . . .

"Every business has their vital few customers, their main customers," says Mene. "They're very loyal, recommend and refer us—they're the core loyalist. In our minds, success is maintaining maximum loyalty from them. Key account customers, as described in the *Mission Statement*, refers to business-to-business customers," he says.

"The *Mission Statement* is seen more as a management guide," according to Mene. "The *Credo* is the worker's compass." The Ritz-Carlton *Credo* is found on wall placards, on wallet-size cards carried by each employee, and it is on display at all meetings just like the flag of the United States.

Employees must be able to recite the *Credo*. In meetings, when the *Credo*'s impact on discussions is questioned, a volunteer will be called upon to recite the *Credo*. "I've yet to find an employee who couldn't recite the *Credo*," says Mene. "Everyone in the company knows it, uses it, and teaches it. The *Credo* hasn't changed in eleven years. New employees receive a two-day orientation program where the *Mission Statement* and the *Credo* are big topics. After orientation and on-the-job training, the employees are then certified as 'quality engineers,' able to spot problems and given the responsibility to solve them."

Each Ritz-Carlton hotel has its employees placed into teams. Each team has to set objectives and come up with plans of action, which are reviewed by the Corporate Steering Committee. Each hotel also has a "quality leader," who oversees the quality plans of each department team.

This dedication to guest satisfaction and detail has paid off. Quarterly guest surveys indicate 98 percent guest satisfaction, the highest in the industry according to the Ritz-Carlton. Following their *Mission Statement* and *Credo* has nabbed them awards such as the Best Hotel Chain in the United States from the Zagat Travel Survey, and they also won the 1992 Malcolm Baldrige National Quality Award. They are the only hotel company to win this award.

A large part of winning this award was Ritz-Carlton's program of Total Quality Management. The president and CEO of The Ritz-Carlton Hotel Company, Horst Schulze, brought this system on board to constantly analyze its product and service so that the customer gets what he or she wants. The system is set up to tell you quickly whether expectations are being met. If they aren't, the system allows for redesigning and modifications. For example, the typical Ritz-Carlton guest is forty years or older and a business leader. Their guest surveys indicate that most would prefer to have written telephone messages rather than an electronic message center. They've told the Ritz-Carlton that they don't want to have voice mail in the hotels. So in most Ritz-Carlton Hotels, the messages are handwritten. They are experimenting in a few hotels with offering the traditional phone message system *and* an electronic message center. The guest can choose either option. The customer doesn't want automated wake-up calls either—they want to hear a real person's voice, so that's what they get.

This level of excellence and attention to customer satisfaction is even carried through to the manner guests are spoken to by a Ritz-Carlton employee. "Good morning" or "Good Evening" are the proper greetings, as well as "Certainly" or "My pleasure" being the proper responses to a request. **A Ritz-Carlton Hotel is a place where the genuine care and comfort of our guests is our highest mission.**

The company motto is "We are ladies and gentlemen serving ladies and gentlemen."

The Ritz-Carlton Hotel Company, headquartered in Atlanta, is a management company that develops and operates luxury hotels for W. B. Johnson Properties. The privately held corporation has been in existence since 1983, when they bought the Ritz-Carlton in Boston and the U.S. rights to the name, originating from owner and renown hotelier César Ritz. In ten years they've grown from one hotel to thirty hotels worldwide with 14,000 employees and plans for major expansion in Europe and Asia.

Because hotels have different needs and circumstances, each is permitted to establish its own mission statement and work toward that goal along with the corporate mission. In addition, some hotels ask individual units to produce mission statements. The engineering department of the Ritz-Carlton in Amelia Island, Florida, had one of the best several years ago: "To boldly go where no hotel has been before— free of all defects."

Ritz-Carlton materials were provided by Ritz-Carlton Hotel Company. Ritz-Carlton is a federally registered trademark of the Ritz-Carlton Hotel Company.

Saturn

Mission

Market vehicles developed and manufactured in the United States that are world leaders in quality, cost and customer satisfaction through the integration of people, technology and business systems and to transfer knowledge, technology and experience throughout General Motors.

We, at SATURN are committed to being one of the world's most successful car companies by adhering to the following values:

COMMITMENT TO CUSTOMER ENTHUSIASM

We continually exceed the expectations of internal and external customers for products and services that are world leaders in cost, quality, and customer satisfaction. Our customers know that we really care about them.

COMMITMENT TO EXCEL

There is no place for mediocrity and half-hearted efforts at SATURN. We accept responsibility, accountability and authority for overcoming obstacles and reaching beyond the best. We choose to excel in every aspect of our business, including return on investment.

TEAMWORK

We are dedicated to singleness of purpose through the effective involvement of members, suppliers, dealers, neighbors and all other stakeholders. A fundamental tenet of our philosophy is the belief that effective teams engage the talents of individual members while encouraging team growth.

TRUST AND RESPECT FOR THE INDIVIDUAL

We have nothing of greater value than our people! We believe that demonstrating respect for the uniqueness of every individual builds a team of confident, creative members possessing a high degree of initiative, self-respect, and self-discipline.

CONTINUOUS IMPROVEMENT

We know that sustained success depends on our ability to continually improve the quality, cost, and timeliness of our products and services. We are providing opportunity for personal, professional, and organizational growth and innovation for all SATURN stakeholders.

Philosophy

We, the Saturn Team, in concert with the UAW and General Motors, believe that meeting the needs of Customers, Saturn Members, Suppliers, Dealers and Neighbors is fundamental to fulfilling our mission.

To meet our customers needs:
- Our products and services must be world leaders in value and satisfaction.

To meet our members needs:
- We will create a sense of belonging in an environment of mutual trust, respect and dignity.
- We believe that all people want to be involved in decisions that affect them, care about their jobs and each other, take pride in themselves and in their contributions and want to share in the success of their efforts.
- We will develop the tools, training and education for each member, recognizing individual skills and knowledge.
- We believe that creative, motivated, responsible team members who understand that change is critical to success are Saturn's most important asset.

To meet our suppliers and dealers needs:
- We will strive to create real partnerships with them.
- We will be open and fair in our dealings, reflecting trust, respect and their importance to Saturn.
- We want dealers and suppliers to feel ownership in Saturn's mission and philosophy as their own.

To meet the needs of our neighbors, the communities in which we live and operate:
- We will be good citizens, protect the environment and conserve natural resources.

- We will seek to cooperate with government at all levels and strive to be sensitive, open and candid in all our public statements.

By continuously operating according to this philosophy, we will fulfill our mission.

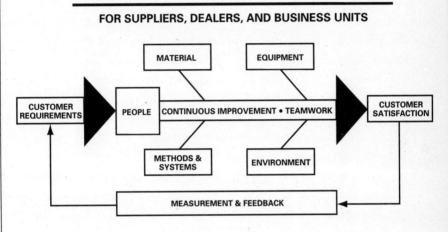

SATURN QUALITY NETWORK

FOR SUPPLIERS, DEALERS, AND BUSINESS UNITS

The workers weren't incompetent, it was the organization.

On February 6, 1984, the historic "Group of 99" was appointed. It was comprised of 99 United Auto Workers union members and General Motors managers and staff from 55 plants. GM recruited all types of personnel from union stewards to assemblers, painters, welders, and plant managers. The main requirement was that the members of the group be people that lived and breathed car production.

The Group of 99 was directed to answer the question: What is it going to take to competitively build a small car in the United States? Their answer was Saturn.

From the beginning, the Group of 99ers understood the importance of a mission statement. "It's important for measurement," says Don Doane, a member of the group and an original Saturn employee. "Whenever there is a decision to be made, we always refer to the *Mission* statement, or the *Philosophy* statement or the *Values* statement." In fact, every department had to develop its own mission statement.

When the topic of employee supervisors came up, the first thing the Saturn leaders did was look at their statements. They found that integrating supervisors into their employee culture contradicted their statements, so they dropped the idea. **We believe that all people want to be involved in decisions that affect them** . . . " 'Manage for efficiency, lead for effectiveness' is one of the phrases used at Saturn," says Doane. "We have leadership training, not management training."

If you visit Saturn's offices in Spring Hill, Tennessee, you'd find that it is practically devoid of traditional business symbols. Employees don't wear ties. The only offices in the building are for the president and the vice presidents. Everyone else has the same size work stations.

Saturn has added the UAW logo on its *Values* statement. "This is one of the unique things about Saturn," says Doane. "The relationship between the union and Saturn is extremely important. Very few decisions are made at Saturn that the union cannot be a part of and very few decisions are made by the union that Saturn cannot be a part of."

Another crucial point in Saturn's mission statement is about accepting change, something that the big three automakers never seem to embrace until it's too late. **We believe that creative, motivated, responsible team members who understand that change is critical to success are Saturn's most important asset.**

Commitment to Customer Enthusiasm is a part of the Saturn *Values* statement. The traditional term used by most car dealers is *customer satisfaction*, but that wasn't good enough at Saturn. "The small-car market was already overcrowded," says Doane. "Satisfying the customer was not enough, so we changed it to *enthusiasm.* Enthusiasm to Saturn means underpromising and overdelivering."

Saturn seems to be achieving their mission. In a recent survey of the National Automotive Dealers Association, Saturn was ranked number one in almost every category. It received *Motor Week*'s 1992 Drivers' Choice Award for Best Small Car for the second year in a row. Saturn began exporting cars to Taiwan in June 1992. In March 1993, according to an industry survey, Saturn averaged 1,072 new car sales per retailer in 1992. Honda was second with 654 per dealer.

And what does General Motors get out of Saturn? Revenue, of course, but much more. Cutting-edge practices, techniques, and processes learned at Saturn will be available to GM, according to the *Mission:* . . . **To transfer knowledge, technology and experience throughout General Motors.**

Saturn was the code name selected for General Motors' small-car project in 1982. Phil Garcia, chief designer in GM's design studio, is credited with the selection of the Saturn name. *Saturn* refers to the Saturn rocket that carried Americans to the moon during the space race with the Soviet Union. The goal of the Saturn project was to design an American vehicle that could beat the Japanese in the small-car race. Having experienced two fuel crises in the late seventies and early eighties, Americans were buying Asian imports that promoted quality, reliability, *and* fuel efficiency.

At this time Ford, GM, and Chrysler, the big American car companies, were losing market share. Because of these losses, GM and the others were closing plants, laying off workers, and experiencing the business nightmare of more supply than demand. The Japanese were building cars in Japan that Americans wanted and doing it for less. GM employees were saying it was one thing to build cars in Japan but let them build plants in America and try to compete. The Japanese built U.S. plants, and they still were the leaders.

Don Ephlin, vice president and director of the United Auto Workers' General Motors Department, and Alfred A. Warren, Jr., vice president of General Motors' industrial relations staff, agreed they had to do something different. GM had a new design for a small car on the drawing board, but, instead of asking the engineers and architects about the car, they decided to take a group of GM personnel that built cars and ask them about building it—the Group of 99.

They were divided into seven small groups pertaining to a certain areas such as the chassis group, the paint and corrosion group, the stamping group, and the HVAC electrical group, and were told that what they had to do was come up with a solution for GM's problem. The Group of 99's seven self-directed teams traveled, interviewed consumers, visited plants, went anywhere, and saw anything they felt pertinent to getting the answer. After two months the group convened and for the next three weeks they studied their research. At first they thought the answer was in technology. But as the groups absorbed the material, they realized technology changed every day and that wasn't the answer. The answer was the structure of the organization.

A representative from each subcommittee would present the concept to the group on what their approach would be and the Group of 99 would approve or veto. If the approach was vetoed, it was back to the drawing board.

Some of the recommendations were that Saturn had to have its own division and identity. It had to be autonomous from the parent, General Motors. It would be doomed to fail if bureaucracy bogged it down. They would have self-directed work teams. They would remove labels, have consensus decision making, and empower employees in decision-making processes. Pretty radical stuff for an automotive manufacturing company.

This information was presented to GM senior management, and on January 7, 1985, GM announced the addition of a new automotive operating unit—the Saturn Corporation, a wholly owned subsidiary company.

The 99ers were all given first option to work at the company they helped create. Don Doane was one who did. Don was a UAW quality worklife coordinator at a GM plant in Ohio who worked on the paint and corrosion subcommittee. He moved to Saturn's new Spring Hill, Tennessee, plant, where today he is a UAW coordinator for sales and service marketing.

Doane was one of those who helped create Saturn's mission statement. It started with creating a mission statement for the group of 99ers. Their mission was "to identify and recommend the best approach to integrate people and technology to competitively manufacture small cars in the U.S."

J. M. Smucker Company

Basic Beliefs

Basic Beliefs are an expression of the Company's values and principles that guide strategic behavior and direction. The Basic Beliefs are deeply rooted in the philosophy and heritage of the Company's founder.

In 1897, the Smucker Company was formed by a dedicated, honest, forward-looking businessman, J. M. Smucker. Because he made a quality product, sold it at a fair price, and followed sound policies, this Company prospered. Today, we who inherit the Smucker name and the Smucker tradition of successful business operations base present policies on these time-honored principles. We interpret them in terms of modern corporate thinking, to be the guideposts of our operations. They are as follows:

QUALITY

Quality applies to our products, our manufacturing methods, our marketing efforts, our people and our relationships with each other. We will only produce and sell products that enhance the quality of life and well-being. These will be the highest quality products offered in our respective markets because Smucker's growth and business success have been built on quality. We will continuously look for ways to achieve daily improvements that will, over time, result in consistently superior products and performance. At Smucker's, quality comes first. Sales growth and earnings will follow.

PEOPLE

We will be fair with our employees and maintain an environment that encourages personal responsibility. In return, we expect our employees to be responsible for not only their individual jobs, but for the Company as a whole. We will seek employees who are committed to preserving and enhancing the values and principles inherent in our Basic Beliefs through their own actions. We firmly believe that:

- Highest quality people produce the highest quality products and service.
- Highest business ethics require the highest personal ethics.
- Responsible people produce exceptional results.

ETHICS

The same, strong ethical values on which our Company was founded and has grown are ingrained in our management team today. This style of management is the standard by which we conduct our business, as well as ourselves. We accept nothing less regardless of the circumstances. Therefore, we will maintain the highest standards of ethics with our shareholders, customers, suppliers, employees, and communities where we work.

GROWTH

Along with day-to-day operations, we are also concerned with the potential of our Company. Growing is reaching for that potential whether it be in the development of new products and new markets, the discovery of new manufacturing or management techniques, or the personal growth and development of our people and their ideas. We are committed to a strong balanced growth that will protect or enhance our consumer franchise within prudent financial parameters. We want to provide a fair return for our stockholders on their investment in us.

INDEPENDENCE

We have a strong commitment to stewardship of the Smucker name and heritage. We will remain an independent company because of our desire and motivation to control our own direction and succeed on our own. We strive to be an example of a company which is successful by operating under these Beliefs within the free enterprise system.

These Basic Beliefs regarding quality, people, ethics, growth and independence have served as a strong foundation in our history. They will continue to be the basis for future strategy, plans and achievements.

Great-grandfather would be proud.

"We get asked all the time, 'Why are you doing as well as you are?' —and we always bring up our *Basic Beliefs*," says Tim Smucker, chairman of the J. M. Smucker Company.

"We don't talk about earnings per share; we don't talk about sales incentives. We talk about *Basic Beliefs*, which come from our past," he says. "We were founded in 1897, and the philosophy of J. M. Smucker, my great-grandfather, was 'Whatsoever man sow, then shall he also reap,' which is certainly the essence of the Golden Rule. You work hard, you treat people right, and the [financial] results will naturally follow. These kinds of beliefs have permeated the company through-out our history."

When Tim Smucker joined the company in 1969, sales were around $50 million and Smucker's had six operations across the United States. Today sales are around half a billion dollars annually from twelve oper-ations in the U.S. and three internationally. "As the company got larger, it was hard to have Dad walking around all the facilities, so we had to decide how to articulate our *Beliefs*," says Smucker. "We de-cided to codify the *Beliefs* we had been living by." His father, Paul, chairman of the executive committee and grandson of the founder, and his brother Richard, president and chief financial officer, comprise the management team, and they wrote the *Beliefs* in the late 1970s.

Quality. "The key thing here is that quality doesn't just apply to the product," says Tim Smucker. "Quality goes throughout all the *Basic Beliefs*. It's how you treat people, it's how you collect numbers, it's how you interact with your customers, your employees. Quality applies to your marketing efforts, to your packaging and your message. You al-ways want to be one hundred percent truthful. In terms of advertising, we don't advertise on game shows or soap operas, because we don't think they are wholesome. We really screen very thoroughly what we want to be associated with, even though we know we're losing money by not advertising on those shows." . . . **quality comes first. Sales growth and earnings will follow.**

People. "When we look for people, it's easy to find people with the skills we need, but it's difficult to find people with the same values," says Smucker. "We don't judge people, but some of the questions we ask are: 'What is important to you? What are your values? Where do they come from? What kind of involvement do you have in your community?' You can really find out what makes somebody tick and if they are the type of person that will make decisions based on the company beliefs."

. . . **we expect our employees to be responsible for not only their individual jobs, but for the Company as a whole.** "We recently added the concept that we should be responsible for everything around us," says Smucker. "The person on the production line has a lot more to do with what goes into the jar than I do or the management does, and so if that person sees something wrong, they now have the responsibility and the authority to communicate their feelings to managers."

Ethics. "Dad said a number of years ago that we wouldn't want to do anything inside the company that we wouldn't feel comfortable saying on national television," says Smucker. "You can't have good company ethics if you don't have good personal ethics. We've put together an ethics training program that we've given to all our employees. We have enough common values—integrity, honesty, and discipline—that always come to the surface. If you're not practicing your ethical fitness when an ethical issues does come up, your decision is harder to make." . . . **we will maintain the highest standards of ethics with our shareholders, customers, suppliers, employees, and communities where we work.**

Growth. "Our philosophy is not to have huge spikes up or down, which means we would never be involved in a fad product," says Smucker. "Jams, jellies, and preserves are the major lines, but we're also leaders in natural peanut butter, fruit syrups, ice cream toppings, and natural juices. We just purchased Mrs. Smith's Pie Company, so we're the leader in frozen pies now. We're in the branded food business—highest quality, and the leader, or a close second." Smucker's has interests in the areas of consumer, food service, industrial, specialty foods, and international foods. Besides Mrs. Smith's Pie Company, some of their well-known brands include The R. W. Knudsen

Family (juices), Santa Cruz Natural (juices), Dickinson's, Lost Acres, and Nice & Natural. "We have some vertical integration," says Smucker. "We do control our source of supply, particularly with fruit."

Independence. "That's a unique one that many companies wouldn't have," says Smucker. "We feel that by staying independent, we're more likely to be able to carry on our *Beliefs*. We have, over the years, been on the screen of a lot of companies. We've never had any direct offers, because we make it well known that the company is not for sale. We do think that family involvement makes a significant impact on the company and the country. Well over fifty percent of the GNP of the United States is from family companies."

The J. M. Smucker Company began in 1897 in Orrville, Ohio, a region known for its agricultural products, including apple orchards planted in part by Jonathan Chapman, also known as Johnny Appleseed. The first products produced by The J. M. Smucker Company were apple cider and apple butter. In those days, to put your name on a product meant you believed in it, guaranteed its quality, and were proud to offer it to your customers. J. M. Smucker took that thought a step further and hand-signed the paper lid on every crock of apple butter he made.

The J. M. Smucker Company *Basic Beliefs* are written on two sides of yellow paper and laminated. All employees have a copy and all new subsidiaries are introduced to the Smucker *Basic Beliefs*. "When we sit down with a new organization that hasn't been a part of the company, we talk about our *Beliefs*," says Smucker. "I tell them that we don't expect them to believe us. I do expect them to test us, to see if we live them. Unless you're understanding them and putting them into practice in your own responsibilities, then they don't mean anything. So we have to live them on a daily basis. We have to continue to reemphasize them time and time again. Every six months we go to all our facilities and talk about the state of the company and thank the people for what they've done. We always talk about our *Basic Beliefs*."

SOUTHLAND'S BUSINESS CONCEPT

"To serve the customer through 7-Eleven stores that achieve a sustainable competitive advantage through superior merchandising... a proprietary process that gives us item-by-item control at each store, providing convenience-oriented customers with what they want...

SPEED... A fast transaction

QUALITY... on those fresh, high-quality products

SELECTION... that they want and need

PRICE... at a fair price

ENVIRONMENT... in a clean, safe, friendly store.

This can only be accomplished through a productive, motivated and efficient organization of franchisees, licensees and employees and with the support of our suppliers and manufacturers."

THE SOUTHLAND CORPORATION
(7-ELEVEN STORES)

CORPORATE MISSION

The Southland Corporation exists to maximize the long-term market value of shareholder equity.

Our heritage is 7-Eleven. Its profitable growth and increasing dominance in convenience retailing will remain the core of our existence. We will be successful to the degree that we fulfill the needs of our customers -- what they want, when and where they want it -- in a manner that provides added value, engenders loyalty and promotes a lasting relationship. To ensure Southland's continued excellence, we must retain the flexibility to anticipate opportunities and master all forms of competitive challenge.

Our most important resource is people. Southland excels because of the quality, motivation and loyalty of every member of the Southland family, franchisee, licensee and employee. We are committed to innovation through participative involvement, and to fostering an environment of trust, respect and shared values.

As a responsible corporate citizen, Southland will conduct its business in an ethical manner with the highest integrity, while contributing to the quality of life in the communities it serves.

The ultimate measure of Southland's success is the optimal utilization of our collective resources and the perpetuation of a culture that is distinguished for its clarity of purpose, emphasis on individual responsibility and standards of excellence.

It's all so simple . . . and fast and convenient, too.

"In my mind, the *Business Concept* is the specific overall strategy," says Clark Matthews, president and chief executive officer of Southland Corporation. "You have a mission against which you test everything you're doing. Then you have certain of the major strategies that are very well defined, that you want everyone to keep in mind specifically, so that the tactics that you implement in order to accomplish the strategies within the mission are consistently being tested," says Matthews.

"It's a three-tiered thing in my mind. The *Business Concept* is much more targeted and focused, whereas the *Corporate Mission* is broader and more global. The majority of the people in the company who are implementing every day need to have something very concise and targeted that they can remember. The *Business Concept* has the five key strategies that fit within the mission statement," he says.

"The mission statement is published for our shareholders, bond-holders, and other stakeholders," says Matthews. "It's constantly referred to by our executive committee as we test whether or not tactics are accomplishing the concept and fit within the overall mission," he says.

Writing the *Business Concept* meant looking at 7-Eleven through the customer's eyes instead of through corporate eyes. "Writing the *Business Concept* involved separating what we wanted versus what the customers wanted," says Cecilia Norwood, vice president for corporate communications. "To step into a store and look at it from the customer's point of view. For example, about one third of our stores sell gasoline. Customers used to have to go into the store to pay and sometimes to have the clerk turn on the pump. Some of the major oil companies started talking about putting point-of-sale systems at the pumps. There was some discussion internally that it was absolutely heretical and would not be done. The whole point was to get the customer into the store to buy other items. The change today is that we now have pay-at-the-pump operations. As we remodel our stores, we remodel the gasoline facilities with better lighting, canopies, faster dispensers, and you can pay at the pump with a credit card. Remember, we're targeting a convenience-oriented customer. They want to find what they want, they don't want to pay too much for it, and they want a speedy transaction." **SPEED . . . A fast transaction.**

Southland Corporation sustains competitive advantage through superior merchandising Norwood relates a saying that is legendary at Southland: "We can't dream up the next Slurpee. Slurpee's almost thirty years old and sales go up every year. It's been a real winner," she says. So instead of trying to dream up the next Slurpee (the company's best-selling frozen, nonalcoholic, flavored beverage), Southland is trying to develop services and service processes to overcome the sudden surges that are associated with products. They're trying to build a merchandising process and decision-making and communication system that will allow their stores to be more responsive to the individual customers in their individual neighborhood in terms of products in stock, brands, variety, and pricing. "It used to be in a 7-Eleven store there wasn't much change in what we sold," says Norwood. "It was an expensive way to operate if we weren't moving merchandise. Now we track the movement of a large percentage of products in each store on an order cycle or a daily basis. After a time, if those products aren't moving, they're deleted from the inventory and we're aggressively replacing them with a selection of new items," she says. **SELECTION . . . that they want and need.**

"That's another philosophical change we've undergone," says Norwood. "In the late eighties, the approach we took with suppliers was that we didn't want their new items in the store until those items had achieved a certain percentage of market share. We wanted a sure thing in the stores. The only problem was by the time the product achieved 'x' share, everyone else had it too. And in many cases it had reached the stage in its life cycle that you had to discount it to move it. Or it was a loss leader in the store," she says. "We've changed that philosophy completely and gone back to our suppliers and said, 'We want to introduce an aggressive, constantly changing selection of new products in our stores every week and we want to assist you with information on our customers so you can develop products that are specifically interesting to our store customers and we want to be the first retailer to have them," she says. This allows Southland to take advantage of manufacturers' introductory advertising campaigns and tagging 7-Eleven as the place to buy the new product.

The five words in the middle of their *Business Concept* were the characteristics they identified after looking through years of major market studies and consumer research that they had at hand. Environment is very important to convenience-oriented customers at 7-Eleven, especially safety. "We've always been in the forefront of the business as far as security programs, and now we're taking another step and upgrading with comprehensive camera systems and personal alarm systems," says Norwood. **ENVIRONMENT . . . in a clean, safe, friendly store.** "When we're remodeling the stores, the single most important thing we're doing is upgrading the lighting inside and outside. It has a fantastic amount to do with not only the walk-up appeal of the store, but how the store feels to be in at certain times of the day, especially to women."

Southland has tried a few new services over the past few years—some worked, some haven't worked. One that didn't work was their video rental section. "We'll never do that again," says Norwood. "To be in the video business and satisfy customers, you really have to have a lot of selection. Trying to check them out at the checkout counter wasn't enhancing the speedy transaction part of the *Business Concept*. It took forever to get a video customer processed, and it angered the other customers," she says. "We couldn't be as competitive as Blockbuster in price, and we weren't enhancing the environment of the store, so it struck out on all counts," she says.

Automatic teller machines, however, are a different matter. "We just signed an agreement last year so we'll have ATM machines in four thousand to fifty-six hundred stores by the end of 1994, and be able to provide a consistent high-quality machine always in service," says Norwood. 7-Eleven will be trying new services in the future, but they'll be sticking to their *Business Concept* when they do it.

"The process that we went through made this a living document that was pertinent on a daily basis to what everybody in the company does to perform their job for the customers," says Matthews. "It's repeated in everything we do, it's talked about in weekly communications conferences. The true test will be in two or three years from now to see if everyone is walking and talking the concept. We do not intend to make a change in strategy. We'll be constantly improving the tactics in order to accomplish the strategies that support the *Corporate Mission*. We believe these strategies are right on for driving the convenience store business in the future," he says.

The Mission Of Southwest Airlines

The mission of Southwest Airlines is dedication to the highest
quality of Customer Service delivered with a sense of warmth,
friendliness, individual pride, and Company Spirit.

To Our Employees

We are committed to provide our employees a stable work
environment with equal opportunity for learning and personal growth.
Creativity and innovation are encouraged for improving the effectiveness
of Southwest Airlines. Above all, employees will be provided the same
concern, respect, and caring attitude within the organization that they are
expected to share externally with every Southwest Customer.

January 1988

SOUTHWEST ®

More than half of the mission statement is about employees.

Southwest Airlines is known for their constantly cheerful and helpful employees. Why are Southwest employees willing to put out so much for their company at a time when some other airlines are faltering?

Ann Rhoades, vice president-people, cites specific aspects of the mission statement for the inspiration. For example: . . . **Customer Service delivered with a sense of warmth, friendliness** . . . Ticketing agents and other employees who deal with customers are permitted to dress casually. It's not unusual to see people dressed in golf shirts and shorts instead of company uniforms.

Says Rhoades: "We tend to hire people with empathy. We want to treat customers as individuals not as numbers on a boarding pass. That's our sense of warmth. When we hire people we ask them to give us an example from their previous job of how they treated a customer who had a problem, how they made it a win-win situation. Most people who have done it in the past will continue to do it in the future. We hire only these people who can give us examples of how they treated customers the way we like them to be treated."

If this seems like so much lip service, Rhoades tells the story about a reservation agent who got a call from a customer who had to fly to a hospital in Houston for cancer treatment, and she had to get there immediately. "The reservation agent found out that the woman had no one to meet her, so she took time to meet the woman when she got off her plane, took her to treatment, and took her back," says Rhoades. "Then she took her again another time and waited for her while she was being operated on."

You can't get much warmer than that.

The company asks a lot of employees—a lot of work and a lot of overtime. "We act as if there is always a financial crisis. We ask employees not to spend extra money unless they have to. We don't have meetings at fancy hotels; we stay in crew hotels. We don't have corporate cars. Even the chairman purchases his own car," says Rhoades. The overtime can be massive because the company has too few people. "We are barely staffed," she says. In fact, Southwest has 86 employees per plane in an industry where the average is 210 employees per plane. "In return for that hard work," says Rhoades, "we promise what we call in the mission statement, **a stable work environment.** The company has never had a furlough or layoff."

Although there is profit sharing and a 401(k) pension plan, employees are rewarded by praise, not money. "We believe people should be proud of their job. We want people to do a job because they feel good about it. It doesn't work to have someone, a boss, stand over them and dictate to them; they have to do it for themselves. You have to want to do it," says Rhoades. "Our mission statement calls that **individual pride.**"

The mission statement also calls for **personal growth,** which is manifested in the company's UP—University for People. Every year employees are given training in improving themselves and their performance. "We want people to grow," says Rhoades. At UP employees are taught how to improve their performance on an individual basis with attention focused on one's weaknesses. Everyone has to learn how to deliver customer service in his or her own way. She says the company also tries to individualize rewards for superb performance and service. "The chairman sends individualized letters to employees' homes to thank them for doing a good job or meeting a certain goal."

"We like our mission statement so much because it spends six lines talking about employees," she says. "You must commit to employees first before they can commit to customers. The customer is not always right, but we make them feel as if they're right."

Southwest Airlines's mission statement was written by its chairman, Herb Kelleher, in 1988 so it could be included in the company's annual report. "It mirrored what we had been doing all along," Rhoades says.

To make sure that employees know their company's mission statement, more than 2,500 copies have been printed and framed and sent into the field. In addition, it's the first thing you see—projected on a movie screen—when you come in for your orientation (or "celebration" as the company calls it) and there's a copy in your new-employee packet. "We sent mission statements out in Cracker Jack boxes to our employees. You know the prize that you get? It was a miniature mission statement."

Southwest Airlines is widely known for the antics of its chairman, who often dresses in clown costumes and regularly boards planes to help flight attendants distribute peanuts ("love bites") and drinks ("love potions"), a reference to home base Dallas's Love Field. The stock symbol is LUV. Kelleher has also dressed as the Easter bunny and bounced down aircraft aisles; one St. Patrick's Day he donned a leprechaun outfit. His skill at remembering employees' names and hosting chili cookouts for workers are known throughout the flying community.

Southwest is also known for making money. In an industry where others are going under, Southwest is growing routes, hiring new people, and making a healthy profit. At the same time, it keeps winning awards: Air Transport World named it 1991 and 1993 Airline of the Year, The International Airline Passengers Association named it 1993's Safest of the World's Biggest Airlines, and the Department of Transportation awarded it the so-called Triple Crown in 1992 and 1993 for best baggage handling, fewest customer complaints, and best on-time performance.

Any new Cracker Jacks offerings in the works? "No," says Rhoades, "but we just put them on mugs. This way you can see it, and so can the person you're talking to."

She adds: "If we see it, we will live it."

Steelcase

Our mission is to provide
the world's best office environment
products, services, systems, and intelligence . . .
designed to help people in offices
work more effectively.

Helping people work more effectively.

What to do when an office is no longer an office.

The new Steelcase mission statement is one sentence long. And it doesn't mention their product, which their former mission statement addressed immediately. "The reason is that the product today may not be the product tomorrow," says Jerry Myers, former president and chief executive officer. "We also see great opportunities in services." They use the word "people" instead of identifying customers and employees. "The beauty of this mission statement is that we can think of it on three levels. One is the vision for the company, the second is that this is an appeal we can make to customers. The third level is inside Steelcase. We want to help our employees work more effectively," he says.

After a lot of debating and arguing, their vision and, thus, their new mission statement was born. **Helping people work more effectively.** "We don't think about it as something that's totally brand new," says Myers. "Everything we've done in our eighty-two-year history has helped people work more effectively, but stating it helps our people broaden their horizons. We need to help companies that are moving toward 'virtual' work. A lot of companies today want their employees to work from their homes, permanently or for part of the week." That's why they don't have references to offices in their new statement.

"We've regarded ourselves for the last dozen years or so as the 'office environment' company. I don't know that we articulated it as the mission, but everybody in the company knew that we were the office environment company with an unwritten subtitle of 'we make great furniture for big companies,'" says Myers.

Steelcase is eighty-seven years old. Their focus has always been on servicing large corporations and selling their products through authorized Steelcase dealers. "That's really what we did, what we focused on," says Myers. "We concentrated on the market that includes very large corporations and sought to satisfy their office furniture needs. That market served us very well during most of the 1970s and 1980s. Our industry was growing during those years at the rate of 20 percent a year, and Steelcase moved from the number-three position in the middle 1960s to the point in 1980 where we were three times as large as anyone else in the business."

They had their first mission statement in the early 1970s. "The old mission statement evolved rather than being formally created," says Myers. Their old mission statement focused on products for the office and helping people in offices work more effectively.

Then came the 1980s. "Our market, like many markets, underwent a major change in the 1980s," says Myers. "The baby boomers were coming into the workforce. We were going from a manufacturing-based economy to a service-based economy. In the late 1960s we had introduced panel-based furniture. With panel-based systems, we tripled our market potential. During the 1970s and 1980s we had an investment tax credit in place in this country that was designed to stimulate purchases of equipment, including panel-based furniture systems. We had tax incentives that stimulated literally hundreds of buildings under construction all over the country, and those buildings needed to be filled with furniture."

In the 1980s, the economy slowed down, commercial construction was close to a standstill, the investment tax credit was gone, and those customers who wanted to convert to panel-based systems had already done so. "What we were finding across the country, and now is starting to happen in Europe and Japan, was that major corporations were restructuring, downsizing, rightsizing, reengineering their businesses, and achieving in the process some tremendous productivity gains," says Myers. "This oftentimes meant fewer white collar workers, which affected our business and the growth of our company."

Steelcase wanted to keep their rate of growth and remain profitable, so in 1992 they hunkered down and examined their situation. "We took an intense look at our industry, our customers, and our company," says Myers. "We asked whether we needed to rethink our focus, and if it had to be changed. And we concluded that it did. The dynamics in our marketplace were changing. Things would never go back to the way they used to be. Our customers today are a lot smarter and a lot more demanding. They want reductions in cycle time; they want reductions in the speed to market with the product; they want even better quality. We always thought we provided the best service in the industry, but customers were saying they wanted us to be more responsive, and they wanted us to be flexible. In many cases, the customers were saying they wanted their product specially engineered for a specific purpose or application. And, of course, they wanted all these things at lower prices."

Over the course of the eighteen-month study period, Steelcase did something a little different. Myers describes the process: "One of the things that we did early on was that we selected two teams of employees outside the management group. These were people that had to be under thirty years of age, bright, with growth potential, and had been with Steelcase fewer than three years. The whole purpose was to get folks that weren't inculturated. We pulled them away from their jobs for six weeks and gave them an assignment. They had to describe Steelcase for us in the year 2005. The only condition given was that between now and 2005, the company was going to grow at the rate of 15 percent or more. They had to talk about the drivers in our market and the surrounding world. They came back six weeks later and addressed the top management group. They told us that to get there we'd have to completely change the way we think about this business; we'd have to change many behaviors and certainly change the paradigms that we're using to guide our decision making and the way we run this outfit. After that process we decided to create fifteen additional teams. The assignment for these teams was to work on a particular project—how we could do a better job in global exploitation, how we could expand into related markets such as medium and small customers. Or they had a specific product or customer and they had to write a business plan. The conventional wisdom at Steelcase had been if you want to do something faster, you should spend more money and put more people on it. What we told these teams was that they had less time, fewer people, and a smaller budget. They got the job done."

Steelcase's board of directors approved this new mission statement in March 1994.

Another unique thing Steelcase did was place an ad in *The Wall*

Street Journal revealing their new mission statement. "We put our new statement in *The Wall Street Journal* as a positioning statement we wanted our customers to see," says Myers.

Myers sees the orientation for employees to the new mission statement as a 12-to-24-month process. "You have to talk about the opportunities it creates," he says. "You have to speak about where we are today and where we want to be. For example, today we would say that one of our competencies is knowledge of office work. As we think about helping people work effectively, no matter when, where, or how, we need knowledge of effective work; we need knowledge of virtual work, we need knowledge of systems integration capability. The whole idea is to liberate our organization so people can think of new businesses and new opportunities. Over this past year we have launched a number of new initiatives that are responsive to this new vision we are creating. For example, we created Turnstone, which sells office products over the phone through a catalog. Another company we've launched is Steelcase Healthcare, which focuses on health care providers and facilities."

The old saying around Steelcase was "stick to your knitting." Myers explains: "What that meant was continue to build great products for big corporations. Don't think about building a work station in a factory. Don't spend a lot of time expanding our lighting business. That's what it meant and it served the company well, because we were on a tear. We couldn't keep up with demand. It was a classic seller's market. 'Sticking to your knitting' doesn't work for us today, because we want our people to think beyond making great products for big companies."

Levi Strauss & Co.

Mission Statement

The mission of Levi Strauss & Co. is to sustain responsible commercial success as a global marketing company of branded casual apparel. We must balance goals of superior profitability and return on investment, leadership market positions, and superior products and service. We will conduct our business ethically and demonstrate leadership in satisfying our responsibilities to our communities and to society. Our work environment will be safe and productive and characterized by fair treatment, teamwork, open communications, personal accountability and opportunities for growth and development.

Aspiration Statement

We all want a Company that our people are proud of and committed to, where all employees have an opportunity to contribute, learn, grow and advance based on merit, not politics or background. We want our people to feel respected, treated fairly, listened to and involved. Above all, we want satisfaction from accomplishments and friendships, balanced personal and professional lives and to have fun in our endeavors. When we describe the kind of LS&CO we want in the future what we are talking about is building on the foundation we have inherited: affirming the best of our Company's traditions, closing gaps that may exist between principles and practices and updating some of our values to reflect contemporary circumstances. What type of leadership is necessary to make our Aspirations a reality?

NEW BEHAVIORS

Leadership that exemplifies directness, openness to influence, commitment to the success of others, willingness to acknowledge our own contributions to problems, personal accountability, teamwork and trust. Not only must we model these behaviors but we must coach others to adopt them.

DIVERSITY

Leadership that values a diverse work force (age, sex, ethnic group, etc.) at all levels of the organization, diversity in experience and a diversity in perspectives. We have committed to taking full advantage of the rich backgrounds and abilities of all our people and to promote a greater diversity in positions of influence. Differing points of view will be sought; diversity will be valued and honesty rewarded, not suppressed.

RECOGNITION

Leadership that provides greater recognition—both financial and psychic—for individuals and teams that contribute to our success. Recognition must be given to all who contribute: those who create and innovate and also those who continually support the day-to-day business requirements.

ETHICAL MANAGEMENT PRACTICES

Leadership that epitomizes the stated standards of ethical behavior. We must provide clarity about our expectations and must enforce these standards throughout the corporation.

COMMUNICATIONS

Leadership that is clear about Company, unit, and individual goals and performance. People must know what is expected of them and receive timely, honest feedback on their performance and career aspirations.

EMPOWERMENT

Leadership that increases the authority and responsibility of those closest to our products and customers. By actively pushing responsibility, trust and recognition into the organization we can harness and release the capabilities of all our people.

Business Vision

We will strive to achieve responsible commercial success in the eyes of our constituencies, which include stockholders, employees, consumers, customers, suppliers and communities. Our success will be measured not only by growth in shareholder value, but also by our reputation, the quality of our constituency relationships, and our commitment to social responsibility. As a global company, our businesses in every country will contribute to our overall success. We will leverage our knowledge of local markets to take advantage of the global positioning of our brands, our product and market strengths, our resources and our cultural diversity. We will balance local market requirements with a global perspective. We will make decisions which will benefit the Company as a whole rather than any one component. We will strive to be cost effective in everything we do and will manage our resources to meet our constituencies' needs. The strong heritage and values of Levi Strauss & Co. as expressed through our Mission and Aspiration Statements will guide all of our efforts. The quality of our products, services and people is critical to the realization of our business vision.

PRODUCTS

We will market value-added, branded casual apparel with Levi's® branded jeans continuing to be the cornerstone of our business. Our brands will be positioned to ensure consistency of image and values to our consumers around the world. Our channels of distribution will support this effort and will emphasize the value-added aspect of our products. To preserve and enhance consumers' impressions of our brands, the majority of our products will be sold through dedicated distribution, such as Levi's® Only-Stores and in-store shops. We will manage our products for profitability, not volume, generating levels of return that meet our financial goals.

SERVICE

We will meet the service commitments that we make to our customers. We will strive to become both the "Supplier of Choice" and "Customer of Choice" by building business relationships that are increasingly inter-dependent. These relationships will be based upon a commitment to mutual success and collaboration in fulfilling our customers' and suppliers' requirements. All business processes in our supply chain—from product design through sourcing and distribution—will be aligned to meet these commitments. Our sourcing strategies will support and add value to our marketing and service objectives. Our worldwide owned and operated manufacturing resources will provide significant competitive advantage in meeting our service and quality commitments. Every decision within our supply chain will balance cost, customer requirements, and protection of our brands, while reflecting our corporate values.

PEOPLE

LS&CO. will be the "Employer of Choice" by providing a workplace that is safe, challenging, productive, rewarding and fun. Our global work force will embrace a culture that promotes innovation and continuous improvement in all areas, including job skills, products and services, business processes, and Aspirational behaviors. The Company will support each employee's responsibility to acquire new skills and knowledge in order to meet the changing needs of our business. All employees will share in the Company's success and commitment to its overall business goals, values and operating principles. Our organization will be flexible and adaptive, anticipating and leading change. Teamwork and collaboration will characterize how we address issues to improve business results.

Values over profits.

In 1985 a group of women and minority managers asked Levi Strauss's CEO Robert Haas for a meeting. They felt there were limited growth opportunities for the groups they represented, and they wanted to make sure that Haas was aware of the situation. The company always had a strong history of equal opportunity and commitment to hiring and promoting minorities compared to other corporations. If you looked at the numbers, things looked pretty good. But something was amiss at the blue jeans giant, and perhaps Haas wasn't seeing what really went on beyond his office walls.

In response, Haas organized a retreat in which ten senior managers —all white males—were teamed up with minority managers in discussion groups. What the senior managers learned was that while the company was doing a good job at equal opportunity based on statistics, numbers were not the whole story. After two and a half days of gut-wrenching talks, the groups concluded that equal opportunity was more a matter of attitude and mindset and that discrimination existed on a subconscious level despite the company's seemingly strong record in that area.

Over the next few years the company held more than a dozen offsite meetings designed to explore the issue of diversity and people's inner prejudices and assumptions based on racial and cultural stereotypes. In 1987 the importance of diversity became one of the company's six aspirations.

"The *Aspiration Statement* reflects basic human values. You don't have to become a different person, you just might have to think a little differently," says Dave Samson, senior manager of corporate communications.

About diversity, the statement says: **Leadership that values a diverse work force (age, sex, ethnic group, etc.) at all levels of the organization, diversity in experience and diversity in perspectives. . . . Differing points of view will be sought; diversity will be values and honesty rewarded, not suppressed.**

But does everyone buy into these beliefs? "You can't train anybody to do anything that he or she doesn't fundamentally believe in," Haas told the *Harvard Business Review* in a story about the company's values. "We've had some very honest discussions where managers say: 'Look, I'm fifty-three years old, and I've managed one way all my life and been successful, and now the company wants me to change. I don't know if I can do it.'"

One of the ways Levi Strauss has chosen to get people to understand and believe its aspirations is through a training program called the "core curriculum." Also known as "leadership week," the seminar is for those at the management level to learn and practice certain aspects of the *Aspiration Statement* including diversity, ethical management practices, communication, and empowerment. Employees under the management level receive a shorter version of the same seminar.

Levi Strauss & Company has a *Mission Statement*, an *Aspiration Statement*, and a *Business Vision*. The *Mission Statement* and the *Aspiration Statement* were put together in late 1986, the *Business Vision* was added in late 1992. "It is the guiding architecture of the company," Samson says. "The *Mission Statement* shows why we're in business; the *Aspiration Statement* shows us how to work with colleagues and partners, and the *Business Vision* shows us where we want to go."

One of the places they didn't want to go was China. In 1993 Levi Strauss announced that it was withdrawing pending contracts in the country due to what it deemed as pervasive human rights violations. This was a tough decision, as China is clearly the fastest-growing market with the largest number of potential consumers in the world. Says Samson: "We did it because we didn't think it was the right place for us." The company nixed trade with China based on their two philosophies. One, in the *Mission Statement* which calls for the company to . . . **sustain responsible commercial success** . . . The second was part of the "global sourcing guidelines," developed from leadership week discussions. This belief is also reflected in the *Business Vision:* **Our success will be measured not only by growth in shareholder value, but also by our reputation, the quality of our constituency relationships, and our commitment to social responsibility.**

Currently, China represents only two percent of Levi's worldwide production, but not having a presence in China in the coming years could hurt future revenues. "We hope the climate improves," says Samson, "but for now we're phasing out our current operations and not signing any new contracts."

Although blue jeans are a worldwide fashion staple, its history is strictly all-American. Levi Strauss arrived in New York City from Bavaria in 1847. He joined his two brothers in the dry goods business, then moved to San Francisco in 1853 to sell to the Gold Rush miners. Levi Strauss learned of the need for rugged pants and, with his experience in handling dry goods, quickly made a pair of pants out of canvas. Levi Strauss dyed the canvas with indigo and added copper rivets and *voilà!* blue jeans were born.

These new pants caught on quickly and soon were the uniform of all who worked outdoors. In 1902, upon his death, the company was inherited by his four nephews, who continued to manufacture blue jeans.

The popularity of the Levi jeans in the 1950s put them up there with baseball, hot dogs, and apple pie. Everyone was wearing Levi's, and this trend continued through the 1960s.

By 1971 the company went public and branched out into other lines of sportswear. By 1985 the company was experiencing losses, however, and the Haas family regrouped, did a 1.65-billion-dollar leveraged buyout, and took the company private.

Today Levi Strauss is the world's number-one producer of brand-name clothing with their Levi's and Britannia lines. They are number two in the domestic jean market in total jeans, and Levi's still scores number one in single brand jean sales. Their Dockers line of casual apparel, introduced in 1986, has been a tremendous success.

Haas is Levi Strauss's great-great-grandnephew and says that he and the company are continuing to deal with the tough issues that the *Aspiration Statement* raises—issues such as China—and using it as the company's guiding beacon.

However, he is not above challenging the *Aspiration Statement*. Several years ago he gave a speech about the *Aspiration* at one of the company's worldwide management meetings. At the conclusion he held up the *Aspiration Statement* and tore it to shreds. "I want each of you to throw away the *Aspiration Statement* and think about what you want for the company and what kind of person you want to be in the workplace and what kind of legacy you want to leave behind. If the result happens to be in the *Aspiration*, that's fine. But if it happens to be something else, the important thing is that you think deeply about who you are and what you stand for. I have enough confidence in your judgment and motivations that I'll go with whatever you come up with."

So far, the *Aspiration Statement* has held firm.

Some Facts About 501 Blue Jeans

- 501 Jeans, which are so popular today, were actually the first blue jean ever made. Created in 1853, the number 501 was picked arbitrarily.
- Levi's makes them in 224 sizes and in 26 different styles. A typical pair uses $1\frac{1}{3}$ yards of denim, 213 yards of thread, 5 buttons, 5 rivets, and one red tab.
- 1.25 million miles of thread are used annually to make 501's. That would wrap around the world more than 50 times.
- The double row of stitching is called "arcuate" and is the oldest apparel trademark, patented in 1873.
- The rear rivets on pockets were removed during the 1930s because of complaints about chafing against school desks and saddles.
- 501's are part of the permanent collection at the Smithsonian Institution.

Statement of Beliefs

WE BELIEVE that both human beings and nature have inherent worth and deserve our respect.

WE BELIEVE in products that are safe, effective, and made of natural ingredients.

WE BELIEVE that our company and our products are unique and worthwhile, and that we can sustain these genuine qualities with an ongoing commitment to innovation and creativity.

WE BELIEVE that we have a responsibility to cultivate the best relationships possible with our co-workers, customers, owners, agents, suppliers and our community.

WE BELIEVE that different people bring different gifts and perspectives to the team and that a strong team is founded on a variety of gifts.

WE BELIEVE in providing employees with a safe and fulfilling work environment, and an opportunity to grow and learn.

WE BELIEVE that competence is an essential means of sustaining our values in a competitive marketplace.

WE BELIEVE our company can be financially successful while behaving in a socially responsible and environmentally sensitive manner.

Mission

TO SERVE our customers by providing safe, effective, innovative, natural products of high quality.

TO BUILD a relationship with our customers that extends beyond product usage to include full and honest dialogue, responsiveness to feedback, and the exchange of information about products and issues.

TO RESPECT, value and serve not only our customers, but also our co-workers, owners, agents, suppliers, and our community; to be concerned about and contribute to their well-being, and to operate with integrity so as to be deserving of their trust.

TO PROVIDE meaningful work, fair compensation, and a safe, healthy work environment that encourages openness, creativity, self-discipline, and growth.

TO CONTRIBUTE to and affirm a high level of commitment, skill and effectiveness in the work community.

TO RECOGNIZE, encourage, and seek a diversity of gifts and perspectives in our worklife.

TO ACKNOWLEDGE the value of each person's contribution to our goals, and to foster teamwork in our tasks.

TO BE DISTINCTIVE in products and policies which honor and sustain our natural world.

TO ADDRESS COMMUNITY CONCERNS, in Maine and around the globe, by devoting a portion of our time, talents, and resources to the environment, human needs, the arts, and education.

TO WORK TOGETHER to contribute to the long-term value and sustainability of our company.

TO BE A PROFITABLE and successful company, while acting in a socially and environmentally responsible manner.

Making your product fit your mission, not the other way around.

"Living the mission" is heard throughout Tom's of Maine. In their business efforts, they keep to the mission by choosing pure, natural ingredients and sensible packaging. **We believe in products that are safe, effective, and made of natural ingredients.** You won't find saccharin, synthetic fragrances, preservatives, artificial flavors, colors, or alcohol in their products. They keep the amount of packaging to a minimum and always try to find recycled, recyclable, and reusable materials. For example, their toothpaste tubes are made entirely of recyclable aluminum. Their cardboard cartons are made from recycled paperboard and printed with soy-based inks. Their glass roll-on deodorant containers are refillable and recyclable. Shampoo bottles are made using recycled milk jugs that are recyclable again. And all their brochures and letterhead are on one-hundred-percent recycled paper. Tom's of Maine products contain no animal ingredients and are tested without using animals. **We believe that both human beings and nature have inherent worth and deserve our respect.** They require a letter from suppliers that none of the ingredients used are tested using animals.

These are all great examples of their mission and beliefs in action, but there have been some problems in adhering to these tough tenets. Tom's of Maine wanted to develop a new deodorant. Previously they had explored different ways to get away from using a petroleum base and go to a more natural base. They finally settled upon a vegetable base, changed the formula, and distributed the new product. "Suddenly consumers were complaining," says Matthew Chappell, son of cofounders Tom and Kate and their only child working in the business. "Instead of making them smell good, around three P.M. they started smelling bad—real bad." It turned out that the vegetable-based deodorant provided an opportunity for additional bacterial growth, emitting a very offensive odor. Tom's determined this new product was not **effective,** as promised in their mission statement, and made the decision to recall $400,000 worth of products. They went back to petroleum-based deodorant which still complied with their mission albeit calling petroleum a natural product is stretching the definition.

Another time Tom's decided to change the deodorant's packaging to employ recyclable plastic. Soon after, they started receiving complaints from consumers about the packaging cracking or the dials on the roll breaking. They determined the recyclable plastic was too soft for the shaping process and had to go back to using nonrecyclable harder plastic. The promise of **high quality** in their *Mission* won out over the promise for **natural products.** Matthew Chappell says they do the best they can, but sometimes they can't do everything they want.

Community service is a large part of their mission and beliefs system. Each year their Community Life Group, composed of employees from various areas, decides where to donate the company's ten percent of pretax profits to the Common Good—charities serving the environment, education, the arts, and human needs. Their employees also are encouraged to use five percent of their paid work time for volunteer activities.

The *Beliefs* call for cultivating the **best relationships possible with . . . customers . . .** For this they have a consumer dialogue team who answer all letters to the company personally and return all phone calls.

Recently, two additions were made to the statements. The first was about competency. Employee competency is important in any business, but when Tom's management proposed adding it to the *Mission*, their 75 full-time employees balked. They felt threatened, because they thought it could be used against them in job evaluations. So, instead, a competency sentence was added to the beliefs statement: **We believe that competence is an essential means of sustaining our values in a competitive marketplace.** And the word **skill** was used in the mission statement: **To contribute to and affirm a high level of commitment, skill and effectiveness in the work community.** The employees felt better with the different shade of meaning.

The second change concerned diversity. The company believed diversity was important in making sure decisions were based on different perspectives, both philosophically and demographically. **We believe** that different people bring different gifts and perspectives to the team and that a strong team is founded on a variety of gifts. And from the *Mission:* **To recognize, encourage, and seek a diversity of gifts and perspectives in our worklife.** To that end, they recently hired an ethno-botanist from Nigeria.

Tom's of Maine was founded by Tom and Kate Chappell twenty-four years ago in Kennebunk, Maine. They are the country's leading maker of natural personal care products, and their toothpaste is the top-selling natural toothpaste in the United States. This $16 million company has enjoyed a five-year compounded annual growth rate of 20 percent and nine consecutive years of profitability.

Although Tom Chappell's business was growing, he still felt something was missing. He decided to attend the Harvard Divinity School, where his search ended when he learned that business didn't have to just be quantitative. He discovered that holding on to his personal values could go along with the growth and financial success of his company. "Values-based businesses captured Tom's eye," says Matthew Chappell.

In 1989, after finishing at Harvard, Tom returned to the company full-time and proposed the idea of a mission statement and a *Statement of Beliefs* to the board and executive team. They liked the idea and worked on it together. When they finished they presented it to all 65 employees for their feedback. The employees could verbally reply or respond in writing on a postcard they were provided. "The problem was language barriers," says Matthew Chappell. "The concepts were not a problem, but the wording just had to be brought into a common language." What emerged was the *Mission* and a *Statement of Beliefs*.

The exact choice of words is crucial to Tom's of Maine's philosophical documents. On the front page of their annual report you'll see: "Like a boater navigating a swirling river with an eye on both shores, Tom's of Maine must steer a middle way between our private aspirations and our ultimate commitment to the common good." It doesn't get more poetic than that.

Twentieth Century Investors

Beliefs That Guide Our Work

- Exceeding the expectations of those we serve.
- Providing the highest quality service.
- Challenging and inspiring the best people.
- Working together as a team.
- Embracing common values.

Team before individual in a high-profile industry.

Jim Stowers, founder and chairman of Twentieth Century Investors, figured writing a corporate mission statement would be easy; it wasn't.

"We set aside two hours every Thursday, and we felt we could just knock this out. There were five of us," Stowers recalls. "It was amazing; we were still there a year later."

The logjam was broken when someone said: "Jim, what are your beliefs? That's what we're really saying."

One of the secrets of Twentieth Century's success is spelled out very clearly in the belief: **Working together as a Team.** While this isn't a new concept in many companies, it is for mutual fund companies, where one person usually calls the shots in each fund. In fact, grandstanding and hotdogging are often encouraged in investment fund managers. "I believe group judgment is better than individual judgment. I learned from myself that I don't know all the answers and I had to have help," says Stowers.

This team approach extends to the company operations as well. The executive management team, headed by Stowers's son, Jim Stowers, III, the president, runs the company on a day-to-day basis.

"One of the greatest things we do in the company is try to get the very best person we can hire. I think of each individual as the link in the chain, and that chain is only as strong as the weakest link, and we can't afford to have a weak link."

Stowers is serious about the team approach. During the weekly sessions to produce the beliefs statement, he was overruled by the group. "I brought up the Golden Rule—Treat people as you would like to be treated—but some people said no, that it has religious connotations.

"As the *Beliefs* say, I believe in **Exceeding the expectations of those we serve,**" says Stowers. "My feeling is people, our shareholders, want to have the best. I didn't say we are the best, but we're trying to be the best. If you admit to yourself that you're not the best but you are trying, you can always improve what you're trying to do."

He adds: "If we make our shareholders successful, they will make us successful. It has to be done in that order. It has to be done for them first."

The same attention is paid to employees, all of whom are listed in the company phone book alphabetically, *by first name*. The *Beliefs* call for **Challenging and inspiring the best people.** "I have to shake everyone's hand when they come into the company. I challenge them when I say: 'We're trying to have the best mutual fund complex. We're trying.'" To this end, the company sends an annual opinion survey to all employees. "We have an outside company that handles these questionnaires; they're done anonymously. We give everyone an opportunity to voice an opinion," says Stowers. "We compare ourselves to previous years, and it give us an indication as to how we're progressing."

"I should have taken the time thirty years ago to write it down," Stowers says of the company's *Beliefs That Guide Our Work*, "but I didn't have time."

Stowers was busy getting the Kansas City mutual investment fund off and running in 1958 with $10,000, most of it borrowed from a local bank. From the start, Stowers's funds operated differently from many other mutual fund operators. He led the way with a policy of investing only in companies with continuously accelerating earnings. He tracked a company's quarterly performance, and if they showed continuous earnings growth, they were a potential buy.

Although this is opposite to many Wall Streeters, who see this as a "following the trend" stance instead of "leading the trend" stance, Stowers says that the system works. The firm's two original funds—Growth Investors and Select Investors—carry two of the best performance records in the industry. Many of its other funds are top performers as well.

The company now manages $27 billion in more than 20 different funds.

Interestingly, Stowers is also criticized for his philosophies of having a "no-minimum" investment policy and not allowing redemptions of more than $250,000 without advance notice. While this favors small investors, sometimes at the expense of potentially larger investors, he stands firm. "I still remember when I was a small investor," says Stowers, who brown-bags it at the company cafeteria almost every day. He believes that fortunes are made by investing for the long term and that anyone can be financially secure if they are determined to do so no matter the size of their beginning nest egg.

There was one other of Stowers's personal beliefs that didn't make the *Beliefs That Guide Our Work*. It's Stowers's staunch conviction in optimism. His saying is: "The best is yet to be." "It's my personal belief that tomorrow is going to be better than today, and I hope that everyone shares my belief." Although it didn't make the company's *Beliefs*, Stowers tries to spread the word wherever he goes.

Authors' Note: Twentieth Century Investors *Beliefs That Guide Our Work* is the most beautiful mission statement we found. The words are accompanied by extraordinary artwork that we could not reproduce adequately.

UPS
##
Corporate Mission and Strategy

UPS CORPORATE MISSION STATEMENT:

- **Customers**—Serve the ongoing package distribution needs of our customers worldwide and provide other services that enhance customer relationships and complement our position as the foremost provider of package distribution services, offering high quality and excellent value in every service.
- **People**—Be a well-regarded employer that is mindful of the well-being of our people, allowing them to develop their individual capabilities in an impartial, challenging, rewarding, and cooperative environment and offering them the opportunity for career advancement.
- **Shareowners**—Maintain a financially strong, manager-owned company earning a reasonable profit, providing long-term competitive returns to our shareowners.
- **Communities**—Build on the legacy of our company's reputation as a responsible corporate citizen whose well-being is in the public interest and whose people are respected for their performance and integrity.

UPS CORPORATE STRATEGY STATEMENT:

UPS will achieve worldwide leadership in package distribution by developing and delivering solutions that best meet our customers' distribution needs at competitive rates. To do so, we will build upon our extensive and efficient distribution network, the legacy and dedication of our people to operational and service excellence, and our commitment to anticipate and respond rapidly to changing market conditions and requirements.

They drive the trucks; the customer drives them.

In the 1980s, UPS was driving into a crossroads.

The world's largest package delivery company was facing changing competition, a growing global marketplace, and customers who were demanding more service than ever before. Although the senior management was beginning to understand all these stresses and threats to the company—and also all the opportunities—some lower-level managers and the rank and file were having a difficult time understanding the upheaval that had befallen their industry.

So in 1989 senior management decided to launch a massive effort to get everyone at UPS to understand that things were not the same in the package delivery business. The "objectives" from the Policy Book, which was the bible for all workers, was being updated. The company would now have a *Corporate Mission Statement* and *Corporate Strategy Statement.*

"The mission statement gave us a direction to go in," says Clinton L. "Bud" Yard, senior vice president of operations. Yard was responsible for assembling a committee to develop a program to communicate the new mission and strategies throughout the company. "We had always thought of ourselves as providing good-quality service. But I think our operations misunderstood the difference between just meeting commitments to deliver the packages and satisfying customers' needs. What we thought was right and the efficient operations we developed to provide that service was not always what the customer wanted or needed. The mission and strategy comments—they go hand in hand—gave us the vision to change. They raised the awareness of everyone."

Developing the *Mission* and *Strategy* took more than a year, and in 1991 it was presented to senior managers worldwide at a conference in April by the managment team that wrote them. By September it was introduced in company publications and a program dubbed Delivering Our Future was begun in 1992. It included a series of half-hour training programs. Salaried workers were paid to attend. They learned about the mission statement, the strategy, the new competitive environment, and the pressures these new changes may cause. It was the first time that such information was ever shared with employees.

One of the main focuses of United Parcel Service's mission statement is on the customer. UPS, for all its excellence in operational aspects of the business, was not as customer-driven as companies around them. Indeed, it was nowhere near its competitors' level of service. The *Strategy* addresses this issue: . . . **by developing and delivering solutions that best meet our customers' distribution needs at competitive rates.** "Customers are an explicitly stated element," says Yard. "We're no longer just putting a product out there. We're creating flexibility in a number of products, because that's what customers are saying they need to run their businesses successfully. The mission statement has led to employee empowerment to identify and serve customers' needs." Yard gave an example of how drivers' rules have changed to accommodate customers. "Before, we might have made one pickup stop at one designated time. Now, if our customers ask a driver to wait a few minutes or come back a bit later, our driver, knowing his or her responsibility is to the customer, can adjust his or her schedule, make a decision to come back, or call back to a manager to get help."

The *Mission Statement* also addresses the needs of people in the company. Although UPS management has enjoyed good relationships with most employees, the relationship with the Teamster drivers has been less than cordial at times. Driver rules and policies are rigid—even down to how fast a driver should walk and in what hand he has to carry the package—and strictly enforced by management. Drivers often think of themselves as having little flexibility and input into how they perform their duties. By sharing with them the company mission and strategy, management hopes to get all employees to understand their roles in an age of customer satisfaction. "In communicating the new mission and strategy, UPSers better understand today's competitive challenges. They understand what it takes to satisfy customer needs and know they are part of a team. We're not asking them to do it alone, but we think we can do it together and we want and value their input," Yard says.

In the two years since the introduction of the "driver sales lead program," drivers generated more than 163,000 leads which have turned into 70,000 new customers. This is the kind of initiative never fostered before the *Mission Statement*.

UPS has a very decentralized structure. Each district controls the pickup, sorting, exchanging, and delivering of packages. As a result, district managers set the tone for their areas. Although UPS as a company has always had its philanthropic side, it was so busy with operational aspects of the company that it may not have been doing enough for some of the individual communities that it served. The *Mission Statement* reaffirms and emphasizes community service with responsibility left to the district manager. **Build on the legacy of our company's reputation as a responsible corporate citizen whose well-being is in the public interest and whose people are respected for their performance and integrity.** "Our people have always cared about the communities they served," says Yard. "Through the *Mission Statement* our district managers have a better understanding of what was expected. . . . Our customers are the businesses that make up the community. So our people see a correlation between giving back to the community and its business benefits. The *Mission Statement* gave our people a better understanding of the company's commitment to community," says Yard.

Some changes at UPS are becoming evident even to noncustomers. The familiar brown trucks—painted that way to emulate the understated elegance of Pullman railroad cars—were recently adorned with maps of the world to show the company's thrust into the global market. There is an 800 number by the map as well. These are the first changes to be seen on the trucks since 1962. "It's following the lead of our customers," says Yard of the move into worldwide delivery. "Their marketplace and service needs are global. We're expanding to meet them."

Worthington Industries

Philosophy

EARNINGS

The first corporate goal for Worthington Industries is to earn money for its shareholders and increase the value of their investment.

We believe that the best measure of the accomplishment of our goal is consistent growth in earnings per share.

OUR GOLDEN RULE

We treat our customers, employees, investors and suppliers as we would like to be treated.

PEOPLE

We are dedicated to the belief that people are our most important asset.

We believe people respond to recognition, opportunity to grow and fair compensation.

We believe that compensation should be directly related to job performance and therefore use incentives, profit sharing or otherwise, in every possible situation.

From employees, we expect an honest day's work for an honest day's pay.

We believe in the philosophy of continued employment for all Worthington people.

In filling job openings every effort is expended to find candidates within Worthington, its divisions or subsidiaries.

When employees are requested to relocate from one operation to another, it is accomplished without financial loss to the individual.

CUSTOMERS

Without the customer and his need for our products and services we have nothing.

We will exert every effort to see that the customer's quality and service requirements are met. Once a commitment is made to a customer, every effort is made to fulfill that obligation.

SUPPLIERS

We cannot operate profitably without those who supply the quality raw materials we need for our products.

From a pricing standpoint we ask only that suppliers be competitive in the marketplace and treat us as they do their other customers.

We are loyal to suppliers who meet our quality and service requirements through all market situations.

ORGANIZATION

We believe in a divisionalized organizational structure with responsibility for performance resting with the head of each operation.

All managers are given the operating latitude and authority to accomplish their responsibilities within our corporate goals and objectives.

In keeping with this philosophy, we do not create corporate procedures. If procedures are necessary within a particular company operation, that manager creates them.

We believe in a small corporate staff and support group to service the needs of our shareholders and operating units as requested.

COMMUNICATION

We communicate through every possible channel with our customers, employees, shareholders and the financial community.

CITIZENSHIP

Worthington Industries practices good citizenship at all levels. We conduct our business in a professional and ethical manner when dealing with customers, neighbors and the general public worldwide.

We encourage all our people to actively participate in community affairs.

We support worthwhile community causes.

The Golden Rule brings in the gold.

"In the mid-seventies I was with the CEO of Dana Corp., Rene McPherson," says John H. McConnell, founder and chairman of the board of Worthington Industries. "He showed me their mission statement. It was a one-page document, and he was very proud of it. So I decided to do one as well," he says. "I didn't believe in corporate policy manuals, but I did believe in a 'set of rules to live by.'"

Earnings come first, according to McConnell. Worthington more than meets their goal of earning money for their shareholders. They achieved record results for both sales and earnings in fiscal 1993. Net sales reached $1.1 billion, 15 percent higher than the previous record set in 1992. According to *Forbes* magazine, their earnings have grown over 250 percent in the past ten years.

Our Golden Rule: "We practice that," says McConnell. "We will remain on top by following the Golden Rule. Generally our philosophy is summed up in two areas: number one, the goal to earn money, and number two, the Golden Rule. We have very good relationships with our customers, our employees, and our suppliers."

People: McConnell says that people make Worthington Industries special, and this is an area where Worthington does things a lot differently from other industrial giants. They pay their employees a salary instead of by the hour as calculated by time clocks. They did away with plant supervisors and said they would not lay off people in bad times.

Worthington Industries has "employee councils." Everyone who is hired, either full- or part-time, has a probationary period, usually around three months. If they've done a good job during that time, someone will bring their name up to the council. The management does not make decisions on permanent hires—the employees do. A potential permanent employee must receive a majority of votes to be awarded permanent status. "If you have a union, you can't have councils," says McConnell, and only 30 percent of our plants are union shops. We feel the employees working with these people in the plant know them better than the foremen do." Once you're in, you're entitled to Worthington's employee benefits such as profit sharing, which is substantial. Typically it equals around 40 percent of an employee's paycheck.

Customers: "If we take care of the customers' needs and quality requirements, they'll do business with us. Otherwise this building will be a pile of rust," says McConnell. According to *Forbes*, Ford has designated Worthington as one of its elite preferred suppliers, because they are quick to respond to its needs.

McConnell had worked for a number of companies before starting Worthington in 1955. "While I was a student at Michigan State, I worked in the Oldsmobile axle plant," he says. "Our group was quicker than the regular employees, so we got the work quota done faster. When we were done, we wanted to study, but the union wouldn't let us study. They wanted us to stretch the work out over the hours of the shift. That's why I decided to put profit sharing into Worthington."

Worthington Industries is a Fortune 500 company and leading manufacturer of metal and plastic products. It operates 31 manufacturing facilities in 11 states and Canada and employs more than 6,500 people. Headquartered in Columbus, Ohio, Worthington has three business segments: processed steel products like flat rolled steel coils to customer specifications and low pressure cylinders; custom products like injection molded plastic parts, and cast products used in rail cars.

The *Philosophy* is bound to stick around despite a change in management. John H. McConnell stepped down from his CEO role in June 1993 and handed the reins to his son, John P. McConnell, who is also the vice chairman.

When questioned in the 1993 annual report about changing the business philosophy, the younger McConnell said: "Absolutely not. The Worthington philosophy is dynamic and adaptable to changing business conditions. We will continue to emphasize communication, motivation, and recognition in working with our people. The ideas of shared profits, decentralized management, line accountability, a small, talented corporate support group, customer service, quality, and, of course, the "Golden Rule" will continue to be at the core of business practices. Our management team is solid and experienced and has helped develop and implement our philosophy. It is not something on the shelf; it is a way of life at Worthington. Our people understand it and have lived it these past thirty-eight years. It will continue to make Worthington Industries far more than just another place to work."

"The key to the whole system is trust," says the elder McConnell. "Our employees trust us. We trust them. We don't lie to them. They don't lie to us."

XEROX

1994 Direction . . .

STRATEGIC DIRECTION:

Xerox, The Document Company, will be the leader in the global document market, providing Document Services that enhance business productivity.

1994 DIRECTION:

We will implement our Strategic Direction by focusing on two vital areas:

OBJECTIVES:

Growth	**Productiveness**
↓	↓

- **Increase customer satisfaction worldwide**
- **Increase market share**

  ↑

- **Increase productivity**
- **Improve ROA**

  ↑

- **Become the benchmark in employee motivation and satisfaction**

- Xerox values
- Our priorities - Customer Satisfaction, Motivation and Satisfaction of Xerox People, Market Share, Return on Assets
- Xerox 2000 - the structural hardware and behavioral software
- Our commitment to Leadership Through Quality

Xerox Values

- We succeed through satisfied customers.
- We aspire to deliver quality and excellence in all that we do.
- We require premium return on assets.
- We use technology to deliver market leadership.
- We value our employees.
- We behave responsibly as a corporate citizen.

"Putting It Together"

EIGHT CULTURAL DIMENSIONS

Market Connected

Action Oriented

Absolute Results Oriented

Line Driven

Team Oriented

Empowered People

Open, Honest Communication

Organization Reflection and Learning

THE XEROX QUALITY POLICY

Xerox is a quality company.

Quality is the basic business principle for Xerox.

Quality means providing our external and internal customers with innovative products and services that fully satisfy their requirements.

Quality improvement is the job of every Xerox employee.

STRATEGIC DIRECTION

Xerox, The Document Company, will be the leader in the global document market, providing Document Services that enhance business productivity.

1994 DIRECTION/OBJECTIVES

We will implement our Strategic Direction by focusing on two vital areas:

Xerox values

Our priorities-Customer Satisfaction, Motivation and Satisfaction of Xerox People, Market Share, Return on Assets

Xerox 2000 - The structural hardware and behavioral software

Our commitment to Leadership Through Quality

How to use benchmarking to succeed.

Xerox is making a strong comeback from the 1980s, when in one year their profits fell 50 percent. Revenues and income are up and they won the prestigious Baldrige Award, the Canadian National Quality Award, and the European Quality Award.

Hector Motroni, vice president of quality and organizational effectiveness, credits their corporate mission statement, the *Direction*, with keeping the company on track. This rather complicated document takes a while for an outsider to decipher, but once figured out, you can see that it's as precise yet as complex as the company itself. And like Xerox, it has lots of layers, but it all works together.

The first part of the *1994 Direction* is the *Strategic Direction*. Calling Xerox the Document Company is the way they now highlight the company's focus. In the past, Xerox had bought into the insurance and finance industries as a way to bolster sagging profits. Now the company is about documents and nothing else. **Xerox, The Document Company, will be the leader in the global document market, providing Document Services that enhance business productivity.** "That part hasn't changed since 1991, when this was adopted," says Motroni. What has changed since then are the *Objectives*. "Our emphasis now is on growth and productiveness." But instead of just saying it, the 1994 *Objectives* use a chart showing the synergy between growth and productiveness which will lead the company to **become the benchmark in employee motivation and satisfaction.**

Benchmarking, a practice brought to the U.S. by Xerox, is a process of measuring your company's processes, services, and practices against the best companies in the world. Benchmarking doesn't necessarily mean comparing your company to your competitors. Generally, companies compare similar processes such as employee compensation, inventory control, and manufacturing techniques against companies that do the same things better than anyone else is the world.

Today Xerox is considered a world leader in benchmarking techniques, and many companies benchmark against them especially in the area of quality.

How will Xerox accomplish their objectives? This is spelled out in the section called *Enablers*. Ironically, the first enabler is the **Xerox Values,** which have been around since the 1940s. It's ironic, because if Xerox had adhered to these six values all along—which includes, among other things, customer satisfaction, quality, and the value of employees—they may have averted their problems in the first place.

Although Motroni would not go so far as to blame straying from the values as the root cause of Xerox's downfall, he admitted that the company's new strategy incorporates the *Values* though in slightly different language.

The second enabler is **Our Priorities:** "Our priorities have changed their order since 1991. It used to be customer satisfaction, return on investment, and then market share. In 1994 it changed to **Customer Satisfaction, Motivation and Satisfaction of Xerox People, Market Share, Return on Assets.** "Everything stems from customer satisfaction," says Motroni, "but we added the part about motivation and satisfaction of Xerox people. If you ask any employee what the priorities are, he or she will know them off the top of their head."

The next enabler is **Xerox 2000—the structural hardware and behavioral software.** Xerox 2000 is the company's vision for, what else, the year 2000. Says Motroni: "We looked at the coming years and said, "what will the environment look like for us?" According to Motroni, Xerox survived the eighties, it will continue to work at being successful in the nineties, but what will the company have to do to succeed beyond? At a senior management meeting in February 1993, CEO Paul Allaire discussed the Xerox 2000 program which was first implemented in 1990 but is changing its emphasis to productivity. "Our focus is to learn how we can achieve world-class productivity. What I'm talking about is the next major step in our journey that started ten years ago this week. . . . We must launch a new crusade to achieve world-class productivity. . . . There are two paths to this goal: The first is breakthrough improvements in our work processes—how we do things. The second is breakthrough improvements in the empowerment of our people—how we engage people."

These can be considered the structural and behavioral software of Xerox 2000.

To summarize, here are the changes that Xerox has undergone so far:

1984 - Leadership through quality
1987 - Customer #1
1990 - Xerox 2000: The Document Company
1992 - Xerox 2000: Putting It Together
1993 - Xerox 2000: World Class Productivity

The last enabler, of course, is **Our commitment to Leadership Through Quality,** a continuing program begun in 1984.

Okay, so how does Xerox use this phalanx of words and phrases they call the *1994 Direction?* Says Motroni: "Every subsequent organizational unit uses it to develop their own objectives and to cascade these objectives down. At any one level our employees can tie what they're doing to what their group's objectives are and what the corporate objectives are. Hence they all feel a sense of connection to the bigger world. It gives them an overall sense as to where they fit in the process. It gives everyone a view of where they fit in the bigger scheme of things. It lets them know that the things that they're working on are important to the corporation. Before this you might be working on something but you didn't know if it was important to the powers that be; you knew it was important to your boss, but you weren't quite sure about anyone else. It also provides a context—the spirit of the company."

The *Direction* also allows employees to feel more secure and empowered: "If you see that the customer comes first and the employees come second, you know what kind of company you're working for. The customer-first thought is very important because it allows people to push back on the system. They feel empowered to say to their boss: 'Here's what you're telling me to do, but it may not be the best for the customer's satisfaction.' When in doubt, you go back to the mission statement," says Motroni.

The *Direction* also allows Xerox people to gauge quantitatively how well they are implementing the company's programs. "All of us sit down once a year and identify the objectives for the coming year, and we track those objectives to the four priorities," says Motroni. "It's in that process that the *Direction* is used. At the end, my boss and I have a piece of paper telling me what I'll be doing for next year. Then at the end of the year, I'll say, 'Here's what I've done,' and I'll be judged on how well I fulfilled the objectives. The *Direction* becomes what each of us has done during the year."

As if this isn't enough, there are a few more aspects to the *Direction* —the *Eight Cultural Dimensions*. "We've started during the last couple of years looking at managers' performance and the other dimension [other than numerical performance] is behavior. We assess managers on how well they've done against the cultural dimensions."

Motroni concedes that to an outsider the *1994 Direction* may seem complex but adds: "These tools have been very effective for us."

Six Rules for Writing and Implementing Your Own Mission Statement

Writing your own mission statement can be a tough job, but ultimately you'll get more out of the assignment than just your mission statement. What you'll end up with is a clear, concise definition of what your company does, how it does it, why it does it, and where it's going in the future. This exercise in itself can help focus your company on the crucial issues that perhaps you didn't realize were there or that you were unwilling to face squarely and honestly.

Each company composes its mission statement in its own way, and this section will give you tips on how to write a mission statement designed for your company. This book is filled with examples of how other companies have done it, and their wisdom and trials can help you to write yours. Read what they've done, and use their techniques when they seem right for you. Be creative; devise and invent methods that suit your company's culture.

Although corporations have used the term "mission statement" to include all kinds of philosophical statements, including missions, values, visions, principles, credos, bonds, and so on, let's break that apart for the moment. For most companies the actual mission statement is short and describes what business they're in and what they do. After that comes the enabling or supporting material—such as values, principles, or philosophies—which helps the company accomplish the mission statement's goals.

The first question you should ask is "What do I want to tell everybody that we do?" For example, Avis's *Quest for Excellence* says: . . . **our business is renting cars** . . . Leo Burnett's mission statement says: **The mission of the Leo Burnett Company is to create superior advertising.**

Although some companies don't have a mission statement, it's helpful for most companies to describe what they do, not just for themselves but for outsiders and investors. For companies going through massive change—such as selling off divisions and focusing only on new core business—having a statement of what they do can be stabilizing and reassuring to employees and investors.

The second part of the project is writing the enablers. These elements tell everyone how the mission statement will be accomplished and what principles or values the company and its people will use to guide them day to day and into the future. This section always evokes strong feelings from executives and others in the company because it's about human values and no two people agree exactly on what these values should be.

A whole or entire mission statement should be as simple or as complex as the company. Look at Steelcase as an example: one sentence says it all. Then look at Xerox. It's so complex that it takes a while to find all the tentacles of this monster. However, each mission statement works for that particular company, and that's what counts.

Intel is a good example of a long mission statement—it has several parts—but because it's laid out in diagram form, it's very simple to comprehend—each section is pithy and to the point.

Rule #1: Keep the statement simple. Not necessarily short, but simple.

Who should write it?

Some mission statements, like the one for Ben & Jerry's, are written by one person. Twentieth Century Investors used a team approach to compose their statement. Other companies, like Boeing and Saturn, used outside assistance when their thoughts and feelings were difficult to articulate.

IBM used a top-down approach—what the CEO wrote becomes dogma. Other CEOs—like Bob Allen of AT&T, who wrote *Our Common Bond*—sent it out for review by employees, then altered it based on their comments.

There is no consensus, but the best approach seems to be that the top manager or managers write the mission statement, then send it out for review and comment by the senior managers and employees. Why? Everyone feels he or she have a hand in producing the document. This involvement helps get people on board. It gets them excited about the document's beliefs and principles. They have a stake in its fulfillment.

And that's **Rule #2: Allow companywide input.**

Sometimes people inside a company are too close to the action to look objectively at the big picture. On the other hand, who knows more about the company than those inside who live it every day? A powerful strategy is to write the mission statement in-house with the help of an outsider. Outsiders bring a fresh perspective to stale problems, and they can help steer around political swamps.

Rule #3: Outsiders can bring clarity and a fresh perspective to your statement-writing process.

What should the mission statement sound like—very proper or colloquial? Northwestern Mutual Life still uses the exact wording of its original statement, written in 1888. Even though some of the phrases are not commonly used anymore, it gives the company the old-fashioned flavor that it relishes and is its strength. The new, fast-moving General Electric uses only three words and one of them is made up—"boundaryless"—to show innovation and a break from the old way of doing business. Hanna Andersson fancies itself a homey, friendly company, and its choice of words reflects warmth and tenderness. The same can be said for Celestial Seasonings.

Rule #4: The wording and tone should reflect the company's personality or what the company would like to be.

After you've written your statement, you're not done. The hardest part lies ahead: dissemination and adoption. How do you get the statement out to workers, and how do you get them to live it?

Getting the word out and in front of workers all the time, making it part of the culture, is a challenge. It's also the part where companies have shown the greatest creativity.

Perhaps the most amusing tack comes from Southwest Airlines. They put their mission statement in boxes of Cracker Jacks and gave them out to employees. When IBM introduced their *Principles*, they not only used their company publications but let managers know that the corporate office would foot the bill for copies to be produced and disseminated to hang in offices around the world. Merck & Co. used a novel approach for dissemination of their *Declaration of Strategic Intent*. It's an actual declaration, signed by all 450 senior managers, framed and hung in all areas.

Wallet-size cards seem to be a good choice for many companies, including Goodyear, Kellogg, The Ritz-Carlton Hotel® Company, Binney & Smith, and Motorola. Many use two versions: one to carry and one to have in the desk or hanging on the wall. Motorola employees use the card for impromptu challenges and games.

Video presentations about the mission statement work well, too, especially when the CEO can't reach everyone personally. Delta Air Lines uses a video presentation, as does Gillette. For companies with many branches, it's the only way the CEO can "visit" them all.

Honda of America teaches courses in the mission statement. United Parcel Service pays hourly workers to attend sessions on their own time so that they can learn about the mission statement.

Rule #5: Share the mission statement in as many creative ways as possible and in as many languages as necessary. Keep it in front of people constantly.

Of course, all of these tips are hollow unless the mission statement is really used.

At many companies, such as Intel and Boeing, all employees, including managers, are judged by how well they follow the mission statement. In many ways this is eminently fair. Everyone knows exactly what is expected of him or her.

The mission statement must continue to be relevant. At Gannett, upper management looks at the *Game Plan* every year to see if it needs updating in a business that changes rapidly. Arthur D. Little also continually checks the company's mission statement to make sure it still makes sense for them.

Many companies have short- and long-term goals in their mission statements. This forces them to visit the statement constantly to see how they're measuring up. Boston Beer Company, for example, has picked 2006 as its date for Samuel Adams to be **the largest and most respected craft or imported beer in the United States.** Other companies call for themselves to be the leader in an industry, and this pledge also invites constant scrutiny of the mission statement.

Lastly, **Rule #6: Rely on the mission statement for guidance. Challenge it continually, and judge employees by how well they adhere to its tenets. Management must say it and live it.**

Reading the mission statements and commentaries in this book, along with the tips presented here, will help you to write your own mission statement, and following your statement will help your company to succeed.

We'd like to hear from you, and we welcome your comments and suggestions. We'd also like to see your mission statement. Please contact us: Patricia Jones and Larry Kahaner, Box 2732, Alexandria, VA 22301. Our fax is 703-548-3182. We're also on Compuserve: 71702,1650; and Internet: lkahaner@access.digex.net.

ABOUT THE AUTHORS

Patricia A. Jones is founder and president of Power Media, a sales and training consultancy, and has spent her career on the business side of the media industry. She worked at Cahners Publishing and Fairchild Publications before moving to broadcasting, where she worked for Metroplex Communications, Legacy Broadcasting, and Group W (Westinghouse) Radio. She has won awards for commercial copy writing, constructed award-winning presentations (including *Billboard*'s Country Music Station of the Year), and produced the first "radiothon" to raise funding for the Vietnam Veterans Memorial. Recently she has consulted on major market broadcast sales and marketing for European broadcasters.

Larry Kahaner is a former Washington reporter for *Business Week* magazine and the author of several nonfiction books, including *On the Line: The Men of MCI Who Took on AT&T and Won* and *Cults That Kill.* He has also authored a mystery novel, *Naked Prey,* under the pseudonym Larry Kane. He has written for the *International Herald Tribune,* the *Washington Post, Omni* magazine, *Popular Science,* and many other publications. Kahaner is a licensed private investigator and owns KANE Associates International, an investigations agency. He has appeared on national TV and radio shows, including CNN's "Larry King Live!," "Evening Magazine," National Public Radio's "All Things Considered," and the "CBS Evening News," as well as on local TV and radio stations in San Francisco, Washington, D.C., New York City, Detroit, St. Louis, Philadelphia, Chicago, Miami, and other cities. He has lectured and given seminars to such diverse groups as police academies, high-technology companies, and universities.

A Note on the Publisher of This Book

This book was published by Currency Doubleday and the following is our corporate mission statement:

Currency's mission is to discover, develop, and promote ideas and practices that link business with life's meaning.

We want to serve our readers and authors by provoking them into new ways of seeing, and living, what is true.

Currency seeks these truths in unconventional places.
We strive to hand the microphone to the most enlightened sources.
In this way, we will continue to challenge our readers to ponder the role of work in their lives.

CURRENCY

DOUBLEDAY